CALIFORNIA NOTARY PUBLIC STUDY GUIDE WITH 7 PRACTICE EXAM

ALL-IN-ONE PREP BOOK INCLUDES:

FULL SUMMARIZATION OF ALL SECTIONS

280 PRACTICE QUESTIONS

100+ TRUE/FALSE QUESTIONS

BOLTON ☙ PREP

TABLE OF CONTENTS

INTRODUCTION

Congratulations on taking the first step towards becoming a notary public in the state of California. This comprehensive guide is your key to success in the California Notary Exam. Crafted by seasoned professionals well-versed in notary public laws, this book is the result of meticulous analysis of past exam papers. By identifying the crucial elements that correlate with exam success, we've distilled the laws and regulations governing these questions into easily digestible outlines.

Our aim is to demystify the complex world of notary public laws, statutes, and legal jargon. We've gone the extra mile to present this information in an unofficial yet simplified manner, making it accessible to all readers. After each section, you'll have the opportunity to test your understanding with true or false questions, reinforcing your knowledge.

After thoroughly absorbing the content in each chapter, you'll be well-prepared to tackle the seven practice tests, comprising a total of 280 multiple-choice questions. These tests will be your invaluable companions on your path to success. We strongly recommend taking your time between each practice test, thoroughly reviewing your answers to ensure you absorb the material effectively.

It's important to note that this book is designed as a valuable companion to the official California Secretary of State publication, the Notary Public Handbook. For the most comprehensive preparation, we strongly recommend reading both resources in tandem. Together, they will equip you to confidently tackle and conquer the California Notary Exam.

The California notary public handbook can be found on the official California Secretary of State website:
https://notary.cdn.sos.ca.gov/forms/notary-handbook-current.pdf

Note

Where gender pronouns appear in this booklet, they are meant to refer to male, female, non-gendered, and nonbinary persons.

GENERAL INFORMATION

APPOINTMENT AND QUALIFICATIONS

To become a notary public, you must meet all of the following requirements:
(Government Code section 8201)

- Be a legal resident of the State of California;
- Be at least 18 years of age;
- Satisfactorily complete a course of study approved by the Secretary of State;
- Pass a written examination prescribed by the Secretary of State; and
- Pass a background check.

To determine if a person meets the requirements to fulfill the responsibilities of the position, a completed application and a 2" x 2" color passport photograph of the applicant shall be submitted at the examination site, then forwarded to the Secretary of State's office and reviewed by Secretary of State staff for qualifying information.

To assist the Secretary of State in determining the identity of an applicant and whether the applicant has been convicted of a disqualifying crime, state law requires all applicants to be fingerprinted as part of a thorough background check prior to being granted an appointment as a notary public. (Government Code section 8201.1) Information concerning the fingerprinting requirements will be mailed to candidates who pass the examination.

SUMMARY

A notary public must:

- Be a legal resident of California; and
- Be at least 18 years of age; and
- Complete a Secretary of State-approved study course; and
- Pass a Secretary of State-approved written exam; and
- Pass a background check.

To see if the Applicant meets the requirements to become a notary public, the Applicant must:

- Complete an application; and
- Obtain a 2" x 2" color passport photograph of themselves; and
- Submit the application and photograph in person at the written examination site.

The Applicant's documentation and photograph are forwarded to the Secretary of State's office to review the Applicant's qualifications. Every Applicant must be fingerprinted to verify identity and conduct a thorough background check for any disqualifying criminal history. Information about fingerprinting requirements will be mailed to all candidates who pass the written examination.

TRUE OR FALSE?

1. A person will become a notary public once they pass a written examination.

✓ Answer key on Page 222

CONVICTIONS

Applicants are required to disclose on their applications all arrests for which trials are pending and all convictions, including convictions that have been dismissed under Penal Code section 1203.4 or 1203.4a. If you have any questions concerning the disclosure of convictions or arrests, contact the Secretary of State's office prior to signing the application. If you do not recall the specifics about your arrest(s) and/or conviction(s), you can contact the California Department of Justice at (916) 227-3849.

The Secretary of State may deny an application for the following reasons:

- Failure to disclose any conviction;
- Conviction of a felony; or
- Conviction of a disqualifying lesser offense.

The applicant has the right to appeal the denial through the administrative hearing process. (Government Code section 8214.3)

For a complete list of reasons the Secretary of State may deny an application, please refer to Government Code section 8214.1. Refer to the Secretary of State's Notary Public Disciplinary Guidelines for a list of the most common disqualifying convictions. The disciplinary guidelines are available on the Secretary of State's website or can be mailed to you upon request.

SUMMARY

Applicants are required to reveal the following on their application:

- Any and all arrests they may have which are awaiting trial; and/or
- Any and all convictions they may have.

This requirement also includes any convictions which have been dismissed under Penal Code section 1203.4 or 1203.4a. If you have any questions about disclosing arrests/convictions, do not sign the application and contact the Secretary of State's office for additional information. If you cannot remember the information about your arrest and/or conviction history, contact the California Department of Justice at (916) 227-3849 for assistance.

The Secretary of State may deny an application due to:

- Failure to disclose any conviction; or
- Conviction of a felony; or
- Conviction of a lesser offense which disqualifies an Applicant.

Applicants may appeal a denial through an administrative hearing process. Government Code section 8214.1 offers a complete list of reasons the Secretary of State may deny an application (https://california.public.law/codes/ca_gov't_code_section_8214.1). Additionally, the Secretary of State's Notary Public Disciplinary Guidelines detail the types of convictions which commonly disqualify an Applicant (https://www.sos.ca.gov/notary/disciplinary-guidelines) or mailed to you upon request.

TRUE OR FALSE?

2. An Applicant does not have to reveal a misdemeanor traffic violation if the fine has been paid in full.

✓ Answer key on Page 222

NOTARY PUBLIC EDUCATION

All persons are required to take and satisfactorily complete a six-hour course of study approved by the Secretary of State prior to appointment as a notary public. Please note that all persons being appointed, no matter how many commission terms held in the past, are required to take the initial six-hour course of study. (Government Code section 8201(a)(3) and (b)).

A notary public who holds a current California notary public commission and who has completed an approved six-hour course at least one time is required to take and satisfactorily complete an approved three-hour refresher course prior to reappointment as a notary public. The three-hour refresher course can only be used to satisfy the education requirement if the notary public is applying for a new commission before their current commission has expired. If the notary public's commission has expired, the individual must satisfactorily complete a six-hour notary public education course before being appointed for another term, even if the individual already once satisfactorily completed an approved six-hour course for a previous commission.

The Secretary of State reviews and approves courses of study. These approved courses include all the material that a person is expected to know to pass the written examination. The Secretary of State compiles a list of all vendors offering an approved course of study. This list is available on the Secretary of State's website or can be mailed to you upon request. (Government Code section 8201.2)

SUMMARY

Applicants must attend and complete a six-hour study program approved by the Secretary of State before they may be appointed, no matter how many commission terms they have held in the past.

If a notary public with a current commission has completed a six-hour study program in the past, the notary public only needs to attend and complete an approved three-hour refresher course prior to their reappointment. The three-hour refresher course is only acceptable if they are applying for the new commission before their current commission has expired. If the individual's commission has already expired, they must attend and complete an approved six-hour study program again even though they have done so in the past.

The Secretary of State reviews and approves all study programs to ensure they contain all the material an Applicant is expected to know to pass the written examination. The Secretary of State maintains a list of all approved study program providers which may be found on the Secretary of State's website at: https://notaryeducation.sos.ca.gov/ or mailed to you upon request.

TRUE OR FALSE?

  3. Every Applicant must attend and complete an approved six-hour study program before

they can be appointed as a notary public.

✓ Answer key on Page 222

REQUIREMENTS AND TIME LIMIT FOR QUALIFYING

Once the commission has been issued, a person has 30 calendar days from the beginning of the term prescribed in the commission to take, subscribe, and file an oath of office and file a $15,000 surety bond with the county clerk's office. The commission does not take effect until the oath and bond are filed with the county clerk's office. The filing must take place in the county where the notary public maintains a principal place of business as shown in the application on file with the Secretary of State. If the oath and bond are not fled within the 30-calendar-day time period, the commission will not be valid, and the person commissioned may not act as a notary public until a new appointment is obtained and the person has properly qualified within the 30-calendar-day time limit. Government Code section 8213(a) permits the filing of completed oaths and bonds by the applicable county clerk by certified mail or other means of physical delivery that provides a receipt. Exceptions are not made to the 30-day filing requirement due to mail service delays, county clerk mail processing delays, or for any other reason. If mailing an oath and bond to the county clerk, sufficient time must be allowed by the newly appointed notary public to ensure timely filing. (Government Code sections 8212 and 8213)

SUMMARY

The notary public has 30 calendar days after the commission has been issued to take, subscribe, and file an oath of office and a $15,000.00 surety bond with the county clerk in the county where the notary public maintains their declared place of business. The commission is not effective until the oath and bond have been filed.

If the oath and bond aren't filed within 30 calendar days, the commission becomes invalid and the person is prohibited from performing any notarial acts. A new appointment must be obtained within the 30 calendar day time limit. Completed oaths and bonds may be filed with the applicable county clerk via certified mail or other physical delivery that provides a receipt. No exceptions to the 30-calendar day deadline will be made for any reason and the newly appointed notary public is responsible for timely filing.

TRUE OR FALSE?

4. A notary public's appointment is valid only if an oath of office and $15,000.00 surety

bond have been filed with the county clerk within 30 calendar days.

✓ Answer key on Page 222

NOTARY PUBLIC BOND

California law requires every notary public to file an official bond in the amount of $15,000. The notary public bond is not an insurance policy for the notary public. The bond is designed only to provide a limited source of funds for paying claims against the notary public. The notary public remains personally liable to the full extent of any damages sustained and may be required to reimburse the bonding company for sums paid by the company because of misconduct or negligence of the notary public. (Government Code sections 8212 to 8214)

SUMMARY

Every California notary public is required to file a $15,000.00 bond. The bond is simply a limited source of funds to pay claims levied against the notary public for misconduct or negligence, not an insurance policy to protect the notary public financially. The notary public is fully liable for any damages arising from the notary public's malpractice including, but not limited to, reimbursement of all funds paid out by the bonding company.

TRUE OR FALSE?

5. A bonding company may file a lawsuit against a notary public for reimbursement of any monies paid out by the bonding company as a result of the notary public's negligence or misconduct.

✓ Answer key on Page 222

GEOGRAPHIC JURISDICTION

A notary public can provide notarial services throughout the State of California. A notary public is not limited to providing services only in the county where the oath and bond are on file. In virtually all of the certificates the notary public is called on to complete, there will be a venue heading such as "State of California, County of ." The county named in the heading in the notarial certificate is the county where the signer personally appeared before the notary public. (Government Code section 8200)

SUMMARY

A notary public may provide notarial services anywhere in California and is not limited to the county where the notary filed the oath and bond. Most certificates presented to the notary public for completion will have the following language in the heading stating:

"State of California, County of _____."

The named county will be the specific California county where the signing party personally appeared before the notary public.

TRUE OR FALSE?

6. A notary public may only notarize documents in the county where their oath and bond are filed.

✓ Answer key on Page 222

ACTS CONSTITUTING THE PRACTICE OF LAW

California notaries public are prohibited from performing any duties that may be construed as the practice of law. Among the acts which constitute the practice of law are the preparation, drafting, or selection or determination of the kind of any legal document, or giving advice in relation to any legal documents or matters. If asked to perform such tasks, a California notary public should decline and refer the requester to an attorney.

SUMMARY

It is unlawful for a California notary public to perform any act that's considered to be an unauthorized practice of law. Such acts include, but are not limited to the following:

- The preparation or drafting of legal documents;
- Selecting any legal document for someone to use; and/or
- Giving legal advice.

If the notary public is asked to perform these services, the notary public should decline and refer the requester to an attorney.

TRUE OR FALSE?

7. A notary public may tell a client which court document they should file and if the client cannot find it, the notary public may prepare the necessary document.

✓ Answer key on Page 222

NOTARY PUBLIC SEAL

Each notary public is required to have and to use a seal. The seal must be kept in a locked and secured area, under the direct and exclusive control of the notary public and must not be surrendered to an employer upon termination of employment, whether or not the employer paid for the seal, or to any other person.

Because of the legal requirement that the seal be photographically reproducible, the rubber stamp seal is almost universal. However, notaries public may use an embosser seal in addition to the rubber stamp. The legal requirements for a seal are shown below. (Government Code section 8207)

The seal must:

- Be photographically reproducible when affixed to a document;
- Contain the State Seal and the words "Notary Public";
- Contain the name of the notary public as shown on the commission;
- Contain the name of the county where the oath of office and notary public bond are on file;
- Contain the expiration date of the notary public's commission;
- Contain the sequential identification number (commission number) assigned to the notary public, as well as the identification number assigned to the seal manufacturer or vendor; and
- Be circular not over two inches in diameter or be a rectangular form of not more than one inch in width by two and one-half inches in length, with a serrated or milled edged border.

Many documents that are acknowledged may later be recorded. A document may not be accepted by the recorder if the notary public seal is illegible. Notaries public are cautioned to make sure that the notary public stamp leaves a clear impression. All the elements must be discernible. The seal should not be placed over signatures or over any printed matter on the document. An illegible or improperly placed seal may result in rejection of the document for recordation and result in inconveniences and extra expenses for all those involved.

The law allows a limited exception when a notary public may authenticate an official act without using an official notary public seal. Because subdivision maps usually are drawn on a material that will not accept standard stamp pad ink and other acceptable inks are not as readily available, acknowledgments for California subdivision map certificates may be notarized without the official seal. The notary public's name, the county of the notary public's principal place of business, and the commission expiration date must be typed or printed below or immediately adjacent to the notary public's signature on the acknowledgment. (Government Code section 66436(c))

A NOTARY PUBLIC SHALL NOT USE THE OFFICIAL SEAL OR THE TITLE NOTARY PUBLIC FOR ANY PURPOSE OTHER THAN THE RENDERING OF NOTARIAL SERVICE. (Government Code section 8207)

A notary public is guilty of a misdemeanor if the notary public willfully fails to keep their notary public seal under the notary public's direct and exclusive control or if the notary public willfully surrenders the notary public's seal to any person not authorized to possess it. (Government Code section 8228.1)

When the notary public commission is no longer valid, the notary public seal must be destroyed to protect the notary public from possible fraudulent use by another. (Government Code section 8207)

SUMMARY

A notary public shall keep a seal that clearly shows the notary's name, the state seal, the words "Notary Public", and the name of the county where the notary's bond and oath are filed. A sequential number identifying the notary and one identifying the vendor shall also be included on the seal. The seal must be clear and dark enough to photocopy legibly and not be any larger than 2" in diameter (circular seal) or no larger than 1" x 2.5" (rectangular seal) with a milled edged border.

The notary public must keep the seal in a locked and secured area under their sole access and control. Failure to do so may result in disciplinary action against the notary public. The notary public is the only owner of their official seal and must never relinquish the seal to anyone, including an employer or former employer. The notary public must destroy their official seal once their commission is no longer active for any reason.

A document with an unclear or poorly placed seal may be rejected by the county recorder, resulting in extra time and expense to correct the defect. To avoid this, the notary public shall make sure their seal is clearly, firmly, and evenly applied and must never obscure text or signatures on the document.

The notary public is always required to authenticate their notarial act by applying their seal to the document. The only exception to this is for notarization of acknowledgments on California subdivision map certificates, which won't accept stamp ink. For these documents, the notary public's name, the county of the notary public's principal place of business, and the commission expiration date must be typed or printed beside or below the notary public's signature.

A NOTARY PUBLIC MUST NEVER USE THEIR OFFICIAL SEAL AND/OR TITLE FOR ANY OTHER PURPOSE THAN PROVIDING NOTARIAL SERVICES.

When the notary public commission is expired or invalid, the seal must be destroyed to prevent fraudulent use by any unauthorized individual.

TRUE OR FALSE?

8. A notary is responsible for the accuracy, clarity, and security of their official seal used for their notarial acts.

✓ Answer key on Page 222

IDENTIFICATION

When completing a certificate of acknowledgment or a jurat, a notary public is required to certify to the identity of the signer of the document. (Civil Code sections 1185(a), 1189, Government Code section 8202) Identity is established if the notary public is presented with satisfactory evidence of the signer's identity. (Civil Code section 1185(a))

Satisfactory Evidence – "Satisfactory Evidence" means the absence of any information, evidence, or other circumstances which would lead a reasonable person to believe that the individual is not the individual he or she claims to be and (A) identification documents or (B) the oath of a single credible witness or (C) the oaths of two credible witnesses under penalty of perjury, as specified below:

A. Identification Documents – The notary public can establish the identity of the signer using identification documents as follows (Civil Code section 1185(b)(3) and (4)):

1. There is reasonable reliance on any one of the following forms of identification, provided it is current or was issued within 5 years:

a. An identification card or driver's license issued by the California Department of Motor Vehicles,

b. A United States passport;

c. An inmate identification card issued by the California Department of Corrections and Rehabilitation, if the inmate is in custody in California state prison, d. Any form of inmate identification issued by a sheriff's department, if the inmate is in custody in a local detention facility; or

2. There is reasonable reliance on any one of the following forms of identification, provided that it also contains a photograph, description of the person, signature of the person, and an identifying number:

(a) A valid consular identification document issued by a consulate from the applicant's country of citizenship, or a valid passport from the applicant's country of citizenship;

(b) A driver's license issued by another state or by a Canadian or Mexican public agency authorized to issue driver's licenses;

(c) An identification card issued by another state;

(d) A United States military identification card (caution: current military identification cards might not contain all the required information);

(e) An employee identification card issued by an agency or office of the State of California, or an agency or office of a city, county, or city and county in California.

(f) An identification card issued by a federally recognized tribal government.

Note: The notary public must include in his or her journal the type of identifying document, the governmental agency issuing the document, the serial or identifying number of the document, and the date of issue or expiration of the document that was used to establish the identity of the signer. (Government Code section 8206(a)(2)(D))

B. Oath of a Single Credible Witness – The identity of the signer can be established by the oath of a single credible witness whom the notary public personally knows. (Civil Code section 1185(b)(1)) The notary public must establish the identity of the credible witness by the presentation of paper identification documents as set forth above. Under oath, the credible witness must swear or affirm that each of the following is true (Civil Code section 1185(b)(1) (A)(i)-(v)):

1. The individual appearing before the notary public as the signer of the document is the person named in the document;
2. The credible witness personally knows the signer;
3. The credible witness reasonably believes that the circumstances of the signer are such that it would be very difficult or impossible for the signer to obtain another form of

identification;

4. The signer does not possess any of the identification documents authorized by law to establish the signer's identity; and
5. The credible witness does not have a financial interest and is not named in the document signed.

Note: The single credible witness must sign the notary public's journal, or the notary public must indicate in his or her journal the type of identifying document, the governmental agency issuing the document, the identifying number of the document, and the date of issuance or expiration of the document presented by the witness to establish the identity of the witness. (Government Code section 8206(a)(2)(D))

C. Oaths of Two Credible Witnesses – The identity of the signer can be established by the oaths of two credible witnesses whom the notary public does not personally know. (Civil Code section 1185(b)(2)) The notary public first must establish the identities of the two credible witnesses by the presentation of paper identification documents as listed above. Under oath, the credible witnesses must swear or affirm under penalty of perjury to each of the things sworn to or affirmed by a single credible witness, as set forth above. (Civil Code sections 1185(b)(2) and 1185(b)(1)(A)(i)-(v))

Note: The credible witnesses must sign the notary public's journal and the notary public must indicate in his or her journal the type of identifying documents, the identifying numbers of the documents, and the dates of issuance or expiration of the documents presented by the witnesses to establish their identities. (Government Code section 8206(a)(2)(E)).

SUMMARY

A notary public certifies the identity of a signer in two steps. First, the notary public must determine there is no reason to suspect the person is misrepresenting their identity. Second, the notary must be presented with one of three things: a valid ID document from the person signing the document; OR the oath of a single credible witness known to the notary public personally; OR the oaths of two credible witnesses if the notary public does not personally know them.

1. Valid ID documents are described in Civil Code sections 1185(b)(3) and (4)).
2. If the person signing the document does not have a valid ID document to present, their identity may be certified by the oath of a single credible witness who personally knows the signer and personally knows the notary public.
   a. The single credible witness must provide the notary public with a valid ID

document establishing their own identification.

    b. The single credible witness must swear under oath that the person signing the document is the person named in the document, AND the person signing the document is personally known to them, AND the person signing the document has no valid ID and cannot reasonably obtain a valid ID, AND the single credible witness is neither named in the document nor has any financial interest in the document.

3. If the person signing the document does not have a valid ID to present and there is no one qualified to act as a single credible witness, their identity may be certified by the oaths of two credible witnesses who personally know the signer.

    a. The two credible witnesses must provide the notary public with valid ID documents establishing their own identities.

    b. The two credible witnesses must swear under oath that the person signing the document is the same person named in the document AND is personally known to both credible witnesses, AND the person signing the document has no valid ID and cannot reasonably obtain a valid ID, AND affirming the two credible witnesses are neither named in the document nor have any financial interest in the document.

4. Any valid ID document presented to the notary public must be current within the past five years; show a photo of the signer; have a physical description of the signer; show a signature of the signer; and have an identification number assigned by the issuing agency.

5. When presented with a valid ID document during a notarial act, the notary public must record the following in their notary journal: the type of valid ID presented; the issuing agency; the identification number assigned by the issuing agency; and the date of issue or expiration.

6. A notary public and/or any witness may not certify a signer's identity if the notary public and/or witness(es) are named in the document or have a financial interest in the document.

TRUE OR FALSE?

9. A witness does not need to present identification to the notary public when swearing under oath to another signer's identity as long as the witness personally knows the notary public very well.

✓ Answer key on Page 222

NOTARY PUBLIC JOURNAL

A notary public is required to keep one active sequential journal at a time of all acts performed as a notary public. The journal must be kept in a locked and secured area (such as a lock box or locked desk drawer), under the direct and exclusive control of the notary public. The journal shall include the items shown below. (Government Code section 8206(a))

- Date, time and type of each official act (e.g., acknowledgment, jurat).
- Character of every instrument sworn to, affirmed, acknowledged or proved before the notary public (e.g., deed of trust)
- The signature of each person whose signature is being notarized.
- A statement that the identity of a person making an acknowledgment or taking an oath or affirmation was based on "satisfactory evidence" pursuant to Civil Code section 1185. If satisfactory evidence was based on:
  1. Paper identification, the journal shall contain the type of identifying document, the governmental agency issuing the document, the serial or identifying number of the document, and the date of issue or expiration of the document;
  2. A single credible witness personally known to the notary public, the journal shall contain the signature of the credible witness or the type of identifying document, the governmental agency issuing the document, the serial or identifying number of the document, and the date of issue or expiration of the document establishing the identity of the credible witness; or
  3. Two credible witnesses whose identities are proven upon the presentation of satisfactory evidence, the journal shall contain the signatures of the credible witnesses and the type of identifying document, the governmental agency issuing the document, the serial or identifying number of the document, and the date of issue or expiration of the document establishing the identity of the credible witnesses.
- The fee charged for the notarial service.
- If the document to be notarized is a deed, quitclaim deed, deed of trust, or other document affecting real property or a power of attorney document, the notary public shall require the party signing the document to place his or her right thumbprint in the journal. If the right thumbprint is not available, then the notary public shall have the party use his or her left thumb, or any available finger and shall so indicate in the journal. If the party signing the document is physically unable to provide a thumb or fingerprint, the notary public shall so indicate in the journal and shall also provide an explanation of that physical condition.

If the sequential journal is stolen, lost, misplaced, destroyed, damaged, or otherwise rendered unusable, the notary public immediately must notify the Secretary of State by certified or registered mail or any other means of physical delivery that provides a receipt. The notification must include the periods of journal entries, the notary public commission number, the commission expiration date, and, when applicable, a photocopy of the police report that lists the journal. (Government Code section 8206(b)).

A notary public must respond within 15 business days after the receipt of a written request from any member of the public for a copy of a transaction in the notary public journal by supplying either a photostatic copy of a line item from the notary public's journal or an acknowledgment that no such line item exists. The written request shall include the name of the parties, the type of document, and the month and year in which the document was notarized. The cost to provide the requested information must not exceed thirty cents ($0.30) per page. (Government Code sections 8206(c) and 8206.5)

The sequential journal is the exclusive property of the notary public and shall not be surrendered to an employer upon termination of employment, whether or not the employer paid for the journal, or at any other time. The circumstances in which the notary public must relinquish the journal or permit inspection and copying of journal transactions and the procedures the notary public must follow are specified in Government Code section 8206(d).

A notary public is guilty of a misdemeanor if the notary public willfully fails to properly maintain the notary public's journal. (Government Code section 8228.1)

Within 30 days from the date the notary public commission is no longer valid, the notary public must deliver all notarial journals, records and papers to the county clerk's office where the oath is on file. If the notary public willfully fails or refuses to do so, the notary public is guilty of a misdemeanor, and shall be personally liable for damages to any person injured by that action or inaction. (Government Code section 8209) Any notarial journals, records and papers delivered to the Secretary of State will be returned to the sender.

SUMMARY

A notary public must maintain only one sequentially numbered notary public journal at a time. The journal must be secured in a locked area only the notary can access and must contain clear details of every notarial act, such as:

- Date, time, and type of each notarial act.
- Nature or title of each document being signed.
- The printed name and signature of each signer.
- Affirmation that the signer's identity was based upon satisfactory evidence and details about the type of satisfactory evidence.
- If the signer's identity is established by paper documentation, the journal must contain

the type of valid ID, the agency that issued the ID, the document ID number assigned by the issuing agency, and the issue or expiration date of the ID.

- If the signer's identity was established by a single credible witness personally known to the notary public, the journal must show the signature of the witness, the type of valid ID document, the agency that issued the document, the document ID or serial number assigned by the issuing agency, and the issue or expiration date of the document.
- If the signer's identity was established by two credible witnesses, the journal must show the signature of each witness, the type of ID documents, the agency that issued the ID documents, the document ID or serial number assigned by the issuing agency, and the issue or expiration date of the document.
- The fee charged for the notarial service.
- If the document to be notarized is a deed, quitclaim deed, deed of trust, or other document affecting real property or a power of attorney document, the signer must also mark their right thumbprint in the journal. If a different finger is used for some reason, the notary public shall note the reason. If the party is unable to provide any thumbprint/fingerprint at all, the notary public shall make a note of the details and explanation of the physical condition preventing the imprint.

If the notary journal is stolen, lost, damaged, or otherwise unusable, the notary public must immediately notify the Secretary of State by certified or registered mail or any physical delivery method that provides a receipt. The notification must include the date range of journal entries, the notary public commission number, the commission expiration date, and, if applicable, a photocopy of the police report regarding a stolen/lost journal.

A notary public has 15 business days to respond to a written request for a copy of any transaction in the notary journal. The request must include the name of the parties, type of document, and the month and year of the notarization. A response shall consist of a photocopy of the pertinent line from the notary public's journal OR a written acknowledgment that no such line item exists. The notary public may not charge more than thirty cents ($0.30) per page to provide the requested information.

The notary public's journal is their sole and exclusive property and must not be surrendered to any party at any time for any reason. The circumstances, which would require a notary public to relinquish their journal or permit its inspection and copying of journal transactions are detailed in Government Code section 8206(d).

A notary public is guilty of a misdemeanor if the notary public fails to properly maintain a notary public journal.

Within 30 days after expiration of a notary public's commission, the notary public must deliver all notarial journals, records, and papers to the county clerk's office where the oath is on file. The notary public is guilty of a misdemeanor offense if they refuse/fail to do so, and shall be personally liable for any damages to any person who may be injured by that failure or refusal.

TRUE OR FALSE?

10. A notary public may maintain two separate notary journals at one time as long as one is for notarial acts at work, and one is for notarial acts outside of work.

✓ Answer key on Page 222

CONFLICT OF INTEREST

A notary public may notarize documents for relatives or others, unless doing so would provide a direct financial or beneficial interest to the notary public. Given California's community property law, care should be exercised if notarizing for a spouse or a domestic partner. A notary public would have a direct financial or beneficial interest to a transaction in the following situations (Government Code section 8224):

- If a notary public is named, individually, as a principal to a financial transaction.
- If a notary public is named, individually, as any of the following to a real property transaction: beneficiary, grantor, grantee, mortgagor, mortgagee, trustor, trustee, vendor, vendee, lessor, or lessee.

A notary public would not have a direct financial or beneficial interest in a transaction if a notary public is acting in the capacity of an agent, employee, insurer, attorney, escrow holder, or lender for a person having a direct financial or beneficial interest in the transaction. If in doubt as to whether or not to notarize, the notary public should seek the advice of an attorney.

SUMMARY

A notary public is allowed to notarize documents for relatives or acquaintances unless doing so would result in direct financial or beneficial interest to the notary public. As such, a notary public therefore may NOT notarize any document in which,

1. The notary public is individually named as a principal party to a financial transaction; and/or
2. The notary public is individually named as a beneficiary, grantor, grantee, mortgagor,

mortgagee, trustor, trustee, vendor, vendee, lessor, or lessee to a real property transaction.

If the notary public is acting in the capacity of an agent, employee, insurer, attorney, escrow holder, or lender, though, he/she receives no direct financial or beneficial interest and may notarize documents for relatives or acquaintances in that capacity.

TRUE OR FALSE?

11. A notary public may notarize the signature of a relative as long as the document being signed doesn't benefit the notary public in any way.

✓ Answer key on Page 222

ACKNOWLEDGMENT

The form most frequently completed by the notary public is the certificate of acknowledgment.

The certificate of acknowledgment must be in the form set forth in Civil Code section 1189. In the certificate of acknowledgment, the notary public certifies:

- That the signer personally appeared before the notary public on the date indicated in the county indicated;
- To the identity of the signer; and
- That the signer acknowledged executing the document.

The notary public sequential journal must contain a statement that the identity of a person making the acknowledgment or taking the oath or affirmation was based on satisfactory evidence. If identity was established based on the oath of a credible witness personally known to the notary public, then the journal must contain the signature of the credible witness or the type of identifying document used to establish the witness' identity, the governmental agency issuing the document, the serial or identifying number of the document, and the date of issue or expiration of the document. If the identity of the person making the acknowledgment or taking the oath or affirmation was established by the oaths or affirmations of two credible witnesses whose identities are proven to the notary public upon the presentation of satisfactory evidence, then the journal must contain the signatures of the credible witnesses and the type of identifying documents, the identifying numbers of the documents, and the dates of issuance or expiration of the documents presented by the witnesses to establish their identities.

The certificate of acknowledgment must be filled completely out at the time the notary public's signature and seal are affixed. The certificate of acknowledgment is executed under penalty of perjury. (Civil Code section 1189(a)(1))

The completion of a certificate of acknowledgment that contains statements that the notary public knows to be false not only may cause the notary public to be liable for civil penalties and administrative action but is also a criminal offense. The notary public who willfully states as true any material fact known to be false is subject to a civil penalty not exceeding $10,000. (Civil Code section 1189(a)(4))

A notary public may complete a certificate of acknowledgment required in another state or jurisdiction of the United States on documents to be fled in that other state or jurisdiction, provided the form does not require the notary public to determine or certify that the signer holds a particular representative capacity or to make other determinations and certifications not allowed by California law.

Any certificate of acknowledgment taken within this state shall be in the following form:

> A notary public or other officer completing this certificate verifies only the identity of the individual who signed the document to which this certificate is attached, and not the truthfulness, accuracy, or validity of that document.

State of California

County of _____ }

   On _____ before me, (here insert name and title of the officer), personally appeared _____

_____

_____

_____ ,

who proved to me on the basis of satisfactory evidence to be the person(s) whose name(s) is/are subscribed to the within instrument and acknowledged to me that he/she/they executed the same in his/her/their authorized capacity(ies), and that by his/her/their signature(s) on the instrument the person(s), or the entity upon behalf of which the person(s) acted, executed the instrument.

I certify under PENALTY OF PERJURY under the laws of the State of California that the foregoing paragraph is true and correct.

WITNESS my hand and official seal.

Notary Public Signature   Notary Public Seal

Note: California notarial law does not provide a provision requiring a California notary public to cross out, or not cross out, pronouns such as he/she/they, on a notarial certificate. An acknowledgment cannot be affixed to a document mailed or otherwise delivered to a notary public whereby the signer did not personally appear before the notary public, even if the signer is known by the notary public. Also, a notary public seal and signature cannot be affixed to a document without the correct notarial wording.

SUMMARY

The most common form completed by the notary public is the certificate of acknowledgment. The certificate of acknowledgment must be in the format found in the official section above. In a certificate of acknowledgment, the notary public certifies that the signer personally appeared before the notary public in a certain county and on a certain date. The notary public certifies the signer and certifies that the signer acknowledged signing the document.

The certificate of acknowledgment must be fully completed when the notary public's signature and seal are added, and it is signed under penalty of perjury.

It is a criminal offense for a notary public to knowingly complete a certificate of acknowledgment containing statements the notary public knows to be false. The notary public may also be liable for civil penalties and administrative action, which is subject to a civil penalty of not more than $10,000.00.

A notary public may complete a certificate of acknowledgment in a different format as required by another state or jurisdiction of the United States, as long as:

1. The document is to be filed in the other state or jurisdiction; and
2. As long as the document does not require the notary public to determine or certify that the signer holds a particular representative capacity or make any other determinations and certifications about the document and/or signer, which is not allowed by California law.

Any certificate of acknowledgment taken within this state shall be in the following form: Reference the form found in the official section.

Note: A notary public cannot complete a certificate of acknowledgment on a document received via mail, delivery, or other means if the signer did not personally appear before the notary public, even if the signer knows the notary public. Additionally, a notary public cannot sign and seal a document without the correct notarial wording.

TRUE OR FALSE?

12.   In a certificate of acknowledgment, the notary public is certifying that the signer proved their identity and acknowledged they signed the document.

✓ Answer key on Page 222

JURAT

The second form most frequently completed by a notary public is the jurat. (Government Code section 8202) The jurat is identified by the wording "Subscribed and sworn to (or affirmed)" contained in the form. In the jurat, the notary public certifies:

- That the signer personally appeared before the notary public on the date indicated and in the county indicated;
- That the signer signed the document in the presence of the notary public;
- That the notary public administered the oath or affirmation*; and
- To the identity of the signer.

Any jurat taken within this state shall be in the following form:

> A notary public or other officer completing this certificate verifies only the identity of the individual who signed the document to which this certificate is attached, and not the truthfulness, accuracy, or validity of that document.

State of California
County of _____

Subscribed and sworn to (or affirmed) before me on this _____ day of _____, 20__, by _____, proved to me on the basis of satisfactory evidence to be the person(s) who appeared before me.

<u>Notary Public Signature</u>   Notary Public Seal

Note: A jurat cannot be affixed to a document mailed or otherwise delivered to a notary public whereby the signer did not personally appear, take an oath, and sign in the presence of the notary public, even if the signer is known by the notary public. Also, a notary public seal and signature cannot be affixed to a document without the correct notarial wording.

*There is no prescribed wording for the oath, but an acceptable oath would be "Do you swear or affirm that the statements in this document are true?" When administering the oath, the signer and notary public traditionally each raise their right hand but this is not a legal requirement.

SUMMARY

The second most frequent form completed by a notary public is the jurat. A jurat is readily identified by the wording "Subscribed and sworn to (or affirmed)" contained in the form's language. In the jurat, the notary public certifies the signer personally appeared before the notary public in the county named in the jurat, on the date shown in the jurat, and that the signer was present and signed the document in the presence of the notary public. The notary public also certifies that they administered the oath or affirmation* and certifies the identity of the signer.

Any jurat taken within this state shall be in the following form:
Reference the form found in the official section above.

Note: A jurat cannot be completed on a document received by the notary public via mail, delivery, or otherwise if the signer did not personally appear before the notary public, take an oath, and sign in the presence of the notary public—even if the signer knows the notary public. Additionally, a notary public cannot sign and seal a document without correct notarial wording.

*There is no prescribed wording for the oath, but an acceptable oath would be "Do you swear or affirm that the statements in this document are true?" When administering the oath, the signer and notary public traditionally each raise their right hand, but this is not a legal requirement.

TRUE OR FALSE?

13.   A jurat requires the signer to swear under oath before the notary public.

✓ Answer key on Page 222

PROOF OF EXECUTION BY A SUBSCRIBING WITNESS

If a person, called the principal, has signed a document but does not personally appear before a notary public, another person can appear on the principal's behalf to prove the principal signed (or "executed") the document. That person is called a subscribing witness. (Code of Civil Procedure section 1935).

A proof of execution by a subscribing witness cannot be used in conjunction with any power of attorney, quitclaim deed, grant deed (other than a trustee's deed resulting from a decree of foreclosure, or a nonjudicial foreclosure pursuant to Civil Code section 2924, or to a deed of reconveyance), mortgage, deed of trust, security agreement, any instrument affecting real property, or any instrument requiring a notary public to obtain a thumbprint from the party signing the document in the notary public's journal. (Government Code section 27287 and

Civil Code section 1195(b)(1) and (2))

The requirements for proof of execution by a subscribing witness are as follows:

- The subscribing witness must prove (say under oath) that the person who signed the document as a party, the principal, is the person described in the document, and the subscribing witness personally knows the principal (Civil Code section 1197); and
- The subscribing witness must say, under oath, that the subscribing witness saw the principal sign the document or in the presence of the principal heard the principal acknowledge that the principal signed the document (Code of Civil Procedure section 1935 and Civil Code section 1197); and
- The subscribing witness must say, under oath, that the subscribing witness was requested by the principal to sign the document as a witness and that the subscribing witness did so (Code of Civil Procedure section 1935 and Civil Code section 1197); and
- The notary public must establish the identity of the subscribing witness by the oath of a credible witness whom the notary public personally knows and who personally knows the subscribing witness. The credible witness must also present to the notary public any identification document satisfying the requirements for satisfactory evidence as described in Civil Code section 1185(b)(3) or (4) (Civil Code section 1196); and
- The subscribing witness must sign the notary public's official journal. The credible witness must sign the notary public's official journal or the notary public must record in the notary public's official journal the type of identification document presented, the governmental agency issuing the document, the serial number of the document, and the date of issue or expiration of the document. (Government Code section 8206(a)(2)(C) and (D))

Note: The identity of the subscribing witness must be established by the oath of a credible witness who personally knows the subscribing witness and who is known personally by the notary public. In addition, the credible witness must present an identification document satisfying the requirements of Civil Code section 1185(b)(3) or (4).

Because proof of execution by a subscribing witness is not commonly used, the following scenario is provided as an example of how proof by a subscribing witness may be used.

The principal, Paul, wants to have his signature on a document notarized. Paul is in the hospital and cannot appear before a notary public. So Paul asks a longtime friend, Sue, to visit the hospital and act as a subscribing witness. When Sue comes to the hospital, Sue must watch Paul sign the document. If Paul has signed the document prior to Sue's arrival, Paul must say (acknowledge) to Sue that Paul signed the document. Then Paul should ask Sue to sign the document as a subscribing witness, and Sue must do so.

Next, Sue must take the document to a notary public. Sue chooses Nancy Notary as the notary public. Sue must bring a credible witness with her to see Nancy Notary. Sue chooses Carl, a longtime friend, as a credible witness because Carl has worked with Nancy Notary for several years. Therefore, Carl can act as Sue's credible witness.

Sue and Carl appear together before Nancy. Nancy determines Nancy personally knows Carl and also examines Carl's California driver's license to establish Carl's identity. Then Nancy puts Carl under oath. Under oath or affirmation, Carl swears or affirms that Carl personally knows Sue, that Sue is the person who signed the document as a subscribing witness, and Carl does not have a financial interest in the document signed by Paul and subscribed by Sue, and is not named in the document signed by Paul and subscribed by Sue. Then Nancy puts Sue under oath. Under oath or affirmation, Sue swears or affirms Sue personally knows Paul, that Paul is the person described as a party in the document, that Sue watched Paul sign the document or heard Paul acknowledge that Paul signed the document, that Paul requested Sue sign the document as subscribing witness and that Sue did so.

Sue signs Nancy's notary public journal as a subscribing witness. Carl must sign Nancy's notary public journal as a credible witness, or Nancy must record in the notary public journal that Carl presented a California Department of Motor Vehicles driver's license, the license number, and the date the license expires. Nancy completes Nancy's notary public journal entry. Nancy then completes a proof of execution certificate and attaches the proof of execution certificate to the document. Sue takes the notarized document back to Paul. A certificate for proof of execution by a subscribing witness shall be in the following form. (Civil Code section 1195)

A notary public or other officer completing this certificate verifies only the identity of the individual who signed the document to which this certificate is attached, and not the truthfulness, accuracy, or validity of that document.

State of California
County of _____ } ss.

On _____ (date), before me,_____ (name and title of officer), personally appeared _____ (name of subscribing witness), proved to me to be the person whose name is subscribed to the within instrument, as a witness thereto, on the oath of _____ (name of credible witness), a credible witness who is known to me and provided a satisfactory identifying document. _____ (name of subscribing witness), being by me duly sworn, said that he/she was present and saw/heard _____ (name[s] of principal[s]), the same person(s) described in and whose name(s) is/are subscribed to the within or attached instrument in his/her/their authorized capacity(ies) as (a) party(ies) thereto, execute or acknowledge executing the same, and that said affiant subscribed his/her name to the within or attached instrument as a witness at the request of _____ (name[s] of principal[s]).
WITNESS my hand and official seal.

Signature _____   (Seal)

Note: California notarial law does not provide a provision requiring a California notary public to cross out, or not cross out, pronouns such as he/she/they, on a notarial certificate. It is not acceptable to affix a notary public seal and signature to a document without the notarial wording.

SUMMARY

If a person has signed a document without a notary, another person may appear before a notary with the signed document on the signer's behalf for proof of execution. In this situation, the signing party is called the "principal" and the person appearing before the notary public on the principal's behalf is called a "subscribing witness".

There are certain documents that cannot use a subscribing witness for proof of signature by the principal, namely: any power of attorney, quitclaim deed, grant deed, mortgage, deed of trust, security agreement, any document affecting real property, and/or any document requiring the notary public to obtain a thumbprint in their notary journal.

The subscribing witness must appear before the notary public with the signed document and verify the principal's signature by doing the following:

- Swear under oath that the principal who signed the document is the same person described in the document, and that the subscribing witness personally knows the principal; and
- Swear under oath that the subscribing witness saw the principal sign the document or heard the principal acknowledge they signed the document; and
- Swear under oath that the principal asked the subscribing witness to co-sign the document as a witness and he/she did so at the principal's request.

The notary public verifies the identity of the subscribing witness based upon an oath made by a separate credible witness who personally knows the notary public and personally knows the subscribing witness. The credible witness must provide the notary public with a valid ID document and sign the notary public's journal. The subscribing witness must also sign the notary public's journal. Certifying a principal's signature using a subscribing witness is not a common situation, so this example has been provided for clarity:

 This is Paul. Paul is in the hospital and wants to sign an auto purchase contract and have it notarized. Paul can't leave the hospital to visit a notary public, so he calls his good friend Sue and asks her to be a subscribing witness to his signature on the auto purchase contract.

 This is Sue. Sue arrives at the hospital and witnesses Paul signing the auto purchase contract. If Paul had signed the contract before Sue's arrival, he would have to affirmatively acknowledge to Sue that he signed the document.

 Paul asks Sue to sign the contract as well, since she is the subscribing witness to his signature on the auto purchase contract.

 Sue takes the signed auto purchase contract to the office of Nancy, a notary public. Sue's friend Carl has worked with Nancy for several years. Since Carl personally knows Sue and personally knows Nancy, Carl is qualified to act as Sue's credible witness.

Nancy personally knows Carl and she examines Carl's driver's license to verify his identity with a valid ID document. Nancy places Carl under oath

 and Carl swears he personally knows Sue, that Sue is the person who signed Paul's auto purchase contract as a subscribing witness, that Carl is not named in the auto purchase contract, and that Carl has no financial or beneficial interest in the auto purchase contract.

 Nancy places Sue under oath and Sue swears she personally knows Paul, AND Paul is the person described in the auto purchase contract, AND Sue watched Paul sign the document (or heard Paul acknowledge that Paul signed the document), AND Paul requested Sue sign the auto purchase contract as a subscribing witness.

 Sue signs Nancy's notary journal as a subscribing witness to Paul's signature. Carl signs Nancy's notary journal as a credible witness to Sue's identity. Nancy records Carl's driver's license data in her notary journal along with any remaining data to be documented. Finally, Nancy completes a proof of execution certificate and attaches it to the auto purchase contract. Sue returns the notarized document to Paul.

TRUE OR FALSE?

14.   A subscribing witness must provide the notary public with one of the following: (1) an identification document for the principal; OR (2) a mutual friend who knows the principal and the notary.

✓ Answer key on Page 222

SIGNATURE BY MARK

When the signer of an instrument cannot write (sign) his or her name, that person may sign the document by mark. (Civil Code section 14) The requirements for notarizing a signature by mark are as follows:

- The person signing the document by mark must be identified by the notary public by satisfactory evidence. (Civil Code section 1185)
- The signer's mark must be witnessed by two persons who must subscribe their own names as witnesses on the document. One witness should write the person's name next to the person's mark and then the witness should sign his or her name as a witness. The witnesses are only verifying that they witnessed the individual make his or her mark on the document.

- A notary public is not required to identify the two persons who witnessed the signing by mark or to have the two witnesses sign the notary public's journal. Exception: If the witnesses were acting in the capacity of credible witnesses in establishing the identity of the person signing by mark, then the witnesses' signatures must be entered in the notary public's journal.
- The signer by mark must include his or her mark in the notary public journal. To qualify as a signature, the making of the mark in the notary public journal, must be witnessed by an individual who must write the person's name next to the mark and then sign his or her own name as a witness.

Following is an example of a document executed by signature by mark:

I, Bob Smith, give my power of attorney to Jane Brown to act as my attorney-in-fact on all matters pertaining to the handling of my estate, finances, and investments. This power of attorney is to remain in effect until another document revoking this instrument has been filed of record thereby rendering this instrument null and void.

Date: <u>Feb. 5, 2013</u> Name: X*Bob Smith* By: *Vicki Jones*
Witness #1

Steve Miller
Witness #2

> A notary public or other officer completing this certificate verifies only the identity of the individual who signed the document to which this certificate is attached, and not the truthfulness, accuracy, or validity of that document.

State of California

County of *Orange* }

On February 5, 2013, before me, John Doe, a notary public, personally appeared <u>Bob Smith</u>, who proved to me on the basis of satisfactory evidence to be the person(s) whose name(s) <u>is</u>/~~are~~ subscribed to the within instrument and acknowledged to me that <u>he</u>/~~she/they~~ executed the same in <u>his</u>/~~her/their~~ authorized capacity(~~ies~~), and that by <u>his</u>/~~her/their~~ signature(s) on the instrument the person(s), or the entity upon behalf of which the person(s) actcd, executed the instrument.

I certify under PENALTY OF PERJURY under the laws of the State of California that the foregoing paragraph is true and correct.

WITNESS my hand and official seal.

<u>Notary Public Signature</u>   Notary Public Seal

Note: California notarial law does not provide a provision requiring a California notary public to cross out, or not cross out, pronouns such as he/she/they, on a notarial certificate. A notary public seal and signature cannot be affixed to a document without the correct notarial wording.

SUMMARY

If a person is unable to write or sign their name on a document, the person may sign the document by mark under the following conditions:

- The notary public must verify the identity of the person signing by mark with satisfactory evidence.
- The signer's mark shall be made in the presence of two additional people who will subscribe their signatures on the document as witnesses. One of the witnesses must print the signer's name next to their mark on the document, then sign their own name in the capacity as a witness. The witnesses are only verifying they observed the person make their mark on the document.
- A notary public is not required to identify the witnesses to a person's mark or record their information/signatures in the notary journal unless said witnesses are present as credible witnesses to verify the identity of the person signing by mark.
- The person signing by mark must also place their mark in the notary public's journal. For the mark to qualify as a valid signature, a witness must observe the person placing their mark in the notary journal. The witness must then print the person's name next to their mark and sign their own name in the notary journal as a witness.

Reference example of a document signed by mark found in the official section above.

TRUE OR FALSE?

15.   Two persons must witness someone making a mark on the document, but they aren't attesting to the person's identity.

✓ Answer key on Page 222

POWERS OF ATTORNEY - CERTIFYING

A notary public can certify copies of powers of attorney. A certified copy of a power of attorney that has been certified by a notary public has the same force and effect as the original power of attorney. (Probate Code section 4307)

A suggested format for the certification is shown below. Other formats with similar wording may also be acceptable.

```
+----------------------------------------------------------------------+
|  State of California          }                                      |
|  County of _____      }                                     |
|                                                                      |
|  I ___(name of notary public)___, Notary Public, certify that on ___(date)___, I examined  |
|  the original power of attorney and the copy of the power of attorney.  I further certify that  |
|  the copy is a true and correct copy of the original power of attorney.  |
|                                                                      |
|  Notary Public Signature                           Notary Public Seal |
+----------------------------------------------------------------------+
```

SUMMARY

A notary public is authorized to certify a copy of a power of attorney if the copy is identical to the original. A notary-certified copy of a power of attorney has the same authority and effect as the original. Reference the form found in the official section above for a suggested sample certification, although other formats with similar wording may also be acceptable.

TRUE OR FALSE?

16.   A notary public can certify a copy of a copy of a power of attorney.

✓ Answer key on Page 222

NOTARIZATION OF INCOMPLETE DOCUMENTS

A notary public may not notarize a document that is incomplete. If presented with a document for notarization, which the notary public knows from his or her experience to be incomplete or is without doubt on its face incomplete, the notary public must refuse to notarize the document. (Government Code section 8205)

SUMMARY

A notary public must refuse to notarize any document which is visibly missing data or information or if the notary knows the document is incomplete based upon their knowledge and experience.

TRUE OR FALSE?

17.   A notary public is allowed to notarize a document with most of the information included plus a couple of blank lines where more information can be added later.

✓ Answer key on Page 222

CORRECTING A NOTARIAL ACT

There are no provisions in the law that allow for the correction of a completed notarial act. If a notary public discovers an error in a notarial act after completing the act, then the notary public should notarize the signature on the document again. All requirements for notarization are required for the new notarial act, including completing and attaching a new certificate containing the date of the new notarial act and completing a new journal entry.

SUMMARY

California law does not allow notarization errors to be corrected once the notarization has been completed. If a notary public learns of a mistake in their notarization, the notary should immediately correct the notarial error and notarize the document again. All requirements for the first notarization still apply to the new notarization, including the completion of a new certificate showing the new notarization date and a new entry in the notary journal.

TRUE OR FALSE?

18.   A notary public has mistakenly misspelled the signer's name when completing a certificate of acknowledgment. When the mistake is brought to the notary public's attention, it is sufficient for the notary to cross out the misspelled name and re-write it correctly with their initials printed next it.

✓ Answer key on Page 222

CERTIFIED COPIES

A notary public may only certify copies of powers of attorney under Probate Code section 4307 and his or her notary public journal. (Government Code sections 8205(a)(4), 8205(b)(1), and 8206(e)). Certified copies of birth, fetal death, death, and marriage records may be made only by the State Registrar, by duly appointed and acting local registrars during their term of office, and by county recorders. (Health & Safety Code section 103545)

SUMMARY

The only document/instrument copies a notary public may certify are powers of attorney and the notary public's own notary journal.

Certified copies of birth, fetal death, death, and marriage records are only made by: (A) the State Registrar; (B) duly appointed and acting local registrars during their term of office; and/or (C) county recorders.

TRUE OR FALSE?

19.   A notary public may compare a copy of someone's birth certificate to the original and notarize a statement that it is a true and accurate copy if the person requesting the certification is named on the birth certificate.

✓ Answer key on Page 222

ILLEGAL ADVERTISING

California law requires any non-attorney notary public who advertises notarial services in a language other than English to post a prescribed notice, in English and the other language, that the notary public is not an attorney and cannot give legal advice about immigration or any other legal matters. The notary public also must list the fees set by statute that a notary public may charge for notarial services. In any event, a notary public may not translate into Spanish the term "Notary Public," defined as "notario publico" or "notario," even if the prescribed notice also is posted. A first offense for violation of this law is grounds for the suspension or revocation of a notary public's commission. A second offense is grounds for the permanent revocation of a notary public's commission. (Government Code section 8219.5)

A notary public legally is barred from advertising in any manner whatsoever that he or she is a notary public if the notary public promotes himself or herself as an immigration specialist or consultant. (Government Code section 8223)

SUMMARY

If a non-attorney notary public advertises notarial services in a language other than English, then the notary public is required by law to post a bilingual notice in English and the other language stating that the notary public is not an attorney and cannot give legal advice of any kind. A list of the statutory fees a California notary public may charge must also be posted. A notary public is prohibited from translating the term "Notary Public," into Spanish (defined as "notario publico" or "notario") even with the mandatory bilingual notice posted. Further, if a notary public advertises as an immigration specialist or consultant, the notary public is legally barred from disclosing their status as a notary public.

A first offense violation of this law may result in immediate suspension or revocation of the notary public's commission. A second offense violation of this law may result in immediate and permanent revocation of the notary public's commission.

TRUE OR FALSE?

20.   A notary public may notarize immigration documents for a signer but may not answer any questions the signer asks about the paperwork.

✓ Answer key on Page 222

IMMIGRATION DOCUMENTS

Contrary to popular belief, there is no prohibition against notarizing immigration documents. However, several laws specifically outline what a notary public can and cannot do. Only an attorney, a representative accredited by the U.S. Department of Justice, or a person who is registered by the California Secretary of State and bonded as an immigration consultant under the Business and Professions Code may assist a client in completing immigration forms. (Business and Professions Code section 22440) A notary public may not charge any individual more than fifteen dollars ($15) for each set of forms, unless the notary public is also an attorney who is rendering professional services as an attorney. (Government Code section 8223)

SUMMARY

A notary public is permitted to notarize immigration documents, but several laws strictly govern the acts a California notary may or may not perform in immigration-related matters. The only professionals allowed to assist a client with completing immigration paperwork are:

1. A licensed attorney; or
2. A representative accredited by the U.S. Department of Justice; or
3. A person who is registered by the California Secretary of State and bonded as an immigration consultant under the Business and Professions Code.

A California notary public may not charge more than fifteen dollars ($15.00) to notarize a set of immigration forms unless the notary public is also an attorney who is rendering professional services as an attorney.

TRUE OR FALSE?

21.   A notary public must voluntarily terminate their notary public commission if the notary public becomes an immigration specialist or consultant.

✓ Answer key on Page 222

CONFIDENTIAL MARRIAGE LICENSES

A notary public who is interested in obtaining authorization to issue confidential marriage licenses may apply for approval to the county clerk in the county in which the notary public resides. A notary public must not issue a confidential marriage license unless he or she is approved by the county clerk having jurisdiction. The county clerk offers a course of instruction, which a notary public must complete before authorization will be granted. Additionally, in order for a notary public to perform the marriage, the notary public must be one of the persons authorized under Family Code sections 400 to 402 (e.g., priest, minister, or rabbi). The county clerk in the county where the notary public resides may or may not approve the authorization to issue confidential marriage licenses. The county clerk should be consulted if the notary public is interested in obtaining approval. (Family Code section 530)

SUMMARY

If a notary public wishes to issue confidential marriage licenses in the county where he/she resides, he/she may apply for approval to the county clerk with proper jurisdiction and complete a mandatory course provided by the county clerk. The county clerk may or may not approve the application, so the notary public is prohibited from issuing confidential marriage licenses until he/she is legally authorized to do so. Additionally, the notary public may not perform any marriage unless he/she is an authorized person as defined by Family Code sections 400 to 402 (priest, minister, rabbi, etc.)

TRUE OR FALSE?

22.   A notary public will be approved to issue confidential marriage licenses once proper application is made with the county clerk and the notary public completes the county

clerk's course of instruction.

✓ Answer key on Page 222

GROUNDS FOR DENIAL, REVOCATION, OR SUSPENSION OF APPOINTMENT AND COMMISSION

The Secretary of State may refuse to appoint any person as notary public or may revoke or suspend the commission of a notary public for specific reasons. These reasons include but are not limited to: a substantial misstatement or omission in the application; conviction of a felony or a disqualifying criminal conviction; failure to furnish the Secretary of State with certified copies of the notary public journal when requested to do so or to provide information relating to official acts performed by the notary public; charging more than the fee prescribed by law; failure to complete the acknowledgment at the time the notary public's seal and signature are attached to the document; executing a false certificate; failure to submit to the Secretary of State any court ordered money judgment, including restitution; failure to secure the sequential journal or the official seal; willful failure to report the theft or loss of the sequential journal; making a false certificate or writing containing statements known to be false; fraud relating to a deed of trust; improper notarial acts; unlawfully acting as a notary; filing false or forged documents; forgery; grand theft; falsely obtaining personal information; willful failure to provide access to a journal when requested by a peace officer; and illegal advertising. (Government Code sections 8205, 8214.1, 8219.5 and 8223)

In addition, the Secretary of State may deny the notary public application or suspend the notary public commission of a person who has not complied with child or family support obligations. (Family Code section 17520)

SUMMARY

The Secretary of State may refuse to appoint any person as a notary public or may revoke or suspend the commission of a notary public for specific reasons including, but not limited to, the following:

- a substantial misstatement or omission in the application;
- conviction of a felony or a disqualifying criminal conviction;
- failure to furnish the Secretary of State with certified copies of the notary public journal when requested to do so or to provide information relating to official acts performed by the notary public;
- charging more than the fee prescribed by law;

- failure to complete the acknowledgment at the time the notary public's seal and signature are attached to the document;
- executing a false certificate;
- failure to submit to the Secretary of State any court ordered money judgment, including restitution;
- failure to secure the sequential journal or the official seal;
- willful failure to report the theft or loss of the sequential journal;
- making a false certificate or writing containing statements known to be false;
- fraud relating to a deed of trust;
- improper notarial acts;
- unlawfully acting as a notary;
- filing false or forged documents;
- forgery;
- grand theft;
- falsely obtaining personal information;
- willful failure to provide access to a journal when requested by a peace officer;
- illegal advertising; and
- non-compliance with child or family support obligations.

TRUE OR FALSE?

23.   The Secretary of State can only refuse to appoint a person as notary public or suspend the active commission of a notary public for the reasons shown in the list.

✓ Answer key on Page 222

DISCIPLINARY GUIDELINES

The Secretary of State's disciplinary guidelines facilitate due process and maintain consistency in reviewing applications, investigating alleged violations, and implementing administrative actions. (Government Code section 8220)

The disciplinary guidelines assist administrative law judges, attorneys, notaries public, notary public applicants, and others involved in the disciplinary process. The disciplinary guidelines are available on the Secretary of State's website or can be mailed to you upon request.

SUMMARY

The Secretary of State's disciplinary guidelines makes sure a notary public or someone applying to be a notary public will receive fairness, consistency, and justice when officials are reviewing applications, investigating alleged violations, and implementing administrative actions. The disciplinary guidelines assist all persons involved in the disciplinary process including the notary applicant or notary public. The disciplinary guidelines are available on the Secretary of State's website or can be mailed to you upon request.

TRUE OR FALSE?

24.   The Secretary of State's disciplinary guidelines makes sure everyone involved in the process of notary approval, investigation, and administrative processes have the same understanding of the process and the notary applicant or notary public is aware of their rights.

✓ Answer key on Page 222

FEES

Government Code section 8211 specifies the maximum fees that may be charged for notary public services. However, a notary public may decide to charge no fee or an amount that is less than the maximum amount prescribed by law. The charging of a fee and the amount of the fee charged is at the discretion of the notary public or the notary public's employer, provided it does not exceed the maximum fees. The notary public is required to make an entry in the notary public journal even if no fee was charged, such as "no fee" or "0." (Government Code section 8206) Exceptions: 1) Pursuant to Government Code section 8203.6, no fees shall be collected by notaries public appointed to military and naval reservations in accordance with 8203.1; 2) Pursuant to Elections Code section 8080, no fee shall be collected by notaries public for verifying any nomination document or circulator's affidavit; 3) Pursuant to Government Code section 6106, no fee shall be collected by a notary public working for a public entity for services rendered in an affidavit, application, or voucher in relation to the securing of a pension; 4) Pursuant to Government Code section 6107, no fee may be charged to a United States military veteran for notarization of an application or a claim for a pension, allotment, allowance, compensation, insurance, or any other veteran's benefits; and 5) Pursuant to Government Code section 8211(d) no fee can be charged to notarize signatures on vote by mail ballot identification envelopes or other voting materials.

In addition, Government Code section 6100 requires any notary public who is appointed to act for and on behalf of certain public agencies, pursuant to Government Code section 8202.5, to charge for all services and remit the fees received to the employing agency. Each fee charged must be entered in the journal.

Note: The maximum fees are as follows.

Service	Description	Maximum Fee
Acknowledgments	Acknowledgment or proof of a deed or other instrument, to include the seal and the writing of the certificate	$15 for each signature
Oaths/Affirmations	Administering an oath or affirmation to one person	$15
Jurats	Executing the jurat including the seal	$15
Deposition Services	All services rendered in connection with taking a deposition. - Administering the oath to the witness - Certificate to the deposition	$30 $7 $7
Voting Materials	Notarize signatures on vote by mail ballot identification envelopes or other voting materials	$0
Powers of Attorney	Certifying a copy of a power of attorney under Probate Code section 4307	$15
Veteran's Benefits	United States military veteran's application or claim for a pension, allotment, allowance, compensation, insurance, or any other veteran's benefit (Government Code section 6107)	$0
Immigration Forms	A notary public qualified and bonded as an immigration consultant may enter data, provided by the client, on immigration forms provided by a federal or state agency	$15 per individual for each set of forms

SUMMARY

The maximum fees a notary public may charge for notarial services are specified in government code, but a notary may choose to charge less than the maximum amount or nothing at all at the discretion of the notary public or their employer but must not exceed the maximum amount. The notary public must record the fee amount in their notary public journal even if no fee was charged, such as "no fee" or "0." and, pursuant to government

code, a notary public may never charge a fee for the following:
If the notary public is appointed to a military or naval reservation;

1. Verifying any nomination document or circulator's affidavit;
2. Working for a public entity for services rendered in an affidavit, application, or voucher in relation to the securing of a pension;
3. Notarizing an application or a claim by a United States military veteran for pension, allotment, allowance, compensation, insurance, or any other veteran's benefits; and
4. Notarizing signatures on vote by mail ballot identification envelopes or other voting materials.

Additionally, any notary public who is appointed to act for and on behalf of certain public agencies much charge for all services and remit the fees received to the employing agency. Each fee charged must be entered in the journal. Reference the fee chart found in the official section above.

TRUE OR FALSE?

25.   A notary public appointed to act on behalf of the Space and Missile Systems Center must charge for all services and remit the fees to the Space and Missile Systems Center.

✓ Answer key on Page 222

CHANGE OF ADDRESS

A notary public is required to notify the Secretary of State of any change of business or residence address in writing, by certified mail or any other means of physical delivery that provides a receipt, within 30 days. (Government Code section 8213.5) Willful failure to notify the Secretary of State of a change of address is punishable as an infraction by a fine of not more than $500. (Government Code section 8213.5)

Upon the change of a business address to a new county, a notary public may elect to file a new oath of office and bond in the new county. However, filing a new oath and bond is optional. Once commissioned, a notary public may perform notary public services anywhere in the state. The original oath and bond must be filed in the county where the notary public's principal place of business is located as shown in the application filed with the Secretary of State. Whether or not a county transfer is filed with the new county after the original oath and bond have been filed in the original county is permissive should the notary public move. (Government Code section 8213) There is no fee for the processing of address change notifications with the Secretary of State.

Note: To ensure proper processing, please include the following information when submitting the written address change notification to the Secretary of State:
Name of the notary public exactly as it appears on the commission certificate;
Commission number and expiration date of the commission;
Whether the address change is for the business, residence, and/or for mailing purposes; and
New business, including business name, residence, and/or mailing address.
Be sure the address change notification is signed and dated by the notary public. The change of address can be submitted in letter form or for convenience, an address change form is available on the Secretary of State's website or can be mailed to you upon request.

SUMMARY

A notary public must notify the Secretary of State of any address change in writing within 30 days and send such notice via certified mail or any delivery method that provides a receipt. Intentional failure to notify the Secretary of State of an address change may be punished by a fine of $500.00.

A notary public is required to have an oath of office and bond filed in the county where their principal place of business is located as reported on their original application, yet the notary public may provide notarial services anywhere in the state. If the notary public's principal place of business changes to a different county, they may choose to file a new oath of office and bond in the new county, but it is not mandatory. There is no fee for processing address change notifications with the Secretary of State.

The notary public's notification of address change to the Secretary of State must include the notary public's name as it appears on their commission certificate; the commission number and expiration date; specify if the change is for business, residence, and/or mailing; and new business name, residence, and/or mailing address. The notification must be signed and dated by the notary public. For convenience, an address change form is available on the Secretary of State's website.

TRUE OR FALSE?

26.   The notary public must file an oath of office and bond in every county where he/she intends to provide notarial services.

✓ Answer key on Page 222

FOREIGN LANGUAGE

A notary public can notarize a signature on a document in a foreign language with which the notary public is not familiar since a notary public's function only relates to the signature and not the contents of the document. The notary public should be able to identify the type of document being notarized for entry in the notary public's journal. If unable to identify the type of document, the notary public must make an entry to that effect in the journal (e.g., "a document in a foreign language"). The notary public should be mindful of the completeness of the document and must not notarize the signature on the document if the document appears to be incomplete. The notary public is responsible for completing the acknowledgment or jurat form. When notarizing a signature on a document, a notary public must be able to communicate with the customer in order for the signer either to swear to or affirm the contents of the affidavit or to acknowledge the execution of the document. An interpreter should not be used, as vital information could be lost in the translation. If a notary public is unable to communicate with a customer, the customer should be referred to a notary public who speaks the customer's language.

SUMMARY

A notary public may notarize a document written in an unfamiliar foreign language only if: (1) the notary public is reasonably sure the document is complete; and (2) the notary public can communicate with the signer well enough to confirm the signer's sworn oath, affirmation, or acknowledgment of their signature. If one or both requirements cannot be met, the notary public must refer the signer to a notary public who speaks the signer's language. An interpreter should not be used since vital details can be lost in the translation. The notary is responsible for completing the acknowledgment or jurat form and if the document has no apparent title, the notary public may simply describe it as "a document in a foreign language" in their notary journal.

TRUE OR FALSE?

27.   A notary public is not required to interpret the foreign language in a document if it looks complete and the notary public can communicate with the signer well enough to confirm their sworn oath, affirmation, and/or acknowledgment of signing.

✓ Answer key on Page 222

ELECTRONIC NOTARIZATIONS

California notaries public are authorized under current law to perform notarizations on documents electronically as long as all the requirements for a traditional paper-based notarial act are met, including the use of a seal for all but two specific documents used in real estate transactions. California law requires a person to appear personally before a notary public to obtain notarial acts like acknowledgments or jurats. This means the party must be physically present before the notary public. A video image or other form of non-physical representation is not a personal appearance in front of a notary public under California State law.

SUMMARY

California notaries are authorized to perform electronic notarizations as long as the usual requirements for a notarization on paper are met in full, including the use of a seal for all types of documents except two specific documents which are used in real estate transactions. The signer is still legally required to appear in person before the notary public for any notarial act like acknowledgments or jurats. A video or other non-physical appearance by the signer does not count as a personal appearance pursuant to state law.

TRUE OR FALSE?

28.   The notary public must file an oath of office and bond in any county where he/she intends to provide notarial services.

✓ Answer key on Page 222

COMMON QUESTIONS AND ANSWERS

Q. My neighbor of 20 years has asked me to notarize a document for her. Because I have known her all these years, do I still need to ask for proof of her identity?
A. Yes. An acknowledgment may not be taken or a jurat executed on the basis of personal knowledge alone. Satisfactory evidence of the signer's identity must be provided and noted in the journal.
Q. I am currently a commissioned notary public applying for reappointment without a break in my commission. Am I still required to submit my fingerprints each time I reapply?
A. Yes. All notary public applicants, whether or not they have held a previous commission, must submit fingerprints to the California Department of Justice for the purpose of a background check. The Department of Justice will forward fingerprint images to the Federal

Bureau of Investigation requesting a federal summary of criminal information that will be provided to the Secretary of State.

Q. If a person was convicted of a DUI, petty theft, trespass, or other crimes, will that person be disqualified from becoming a notary public?

A. The Secretary of State cannot make a determination as to whether or not a person meets the qualifications to become a notary public until a thorough background check has been completed. If you are concerned as to whether you may be disqualified from becoming a notary public based upon past conviction information, please refer to the Secretary of State's Notary Public Disciplinary Guidelines, which also include a list of the most common disqualifying convictions. The disciplinary guidelines are available on the Secretary of State's website or can be mailed to you upon request.

Q. I had a conviction over 25 years ago. Do I still need to disclose this conviction on my application?

A. Yes. There is no time limit for disclosure of convictions. If you have ever been convicted, including a conviction for a DUI, you must disclose the conviction on your application. Failure to disclose all conviction information on each application for an appointment or reappointment is grounds for denial.

Q. How soon can I take the test for reappointment if I currently hold a notary public commission?

A. To avoid a break in commission terms, you should take the exam at least six months prior to the expiration date of your current commission. Test results are valid for one year from the date of the examination. (Title 2, California Code of Regulations, section 20803)

Q. Will I be required to take an approved course of study each time I apply for reappointment?

A. Yes. An applicant for notary public who holds a California notary public commission and who has completed the initial six-hour course of study from an approved vendor will be required to complete a three-hour refresher course of study from an approved vendor prior to reappointment as a notary public for all subsequent terms. In order to meet the requirement to take the three-hour refresher course, a person must apply for reappointment before the current commission expires. An applicant whose commission expires before application is made for a new commission must take an approved six-hour course, even if the applicant previously has completed an approved six-hour course. (Government Code section 8201(b)(2))

Q. I have completed my approved six-hour course of study and received my proof of completion certificate. What do I do with it?

A. Once you have completed your six-hour course of study from an approved vendor, staple your proof of completion certificate to the application and take both items with you to the exam.

Q. Can a six-hour notary public education course be taken in place of a three-hour refresher course?

A. Yes. A six-hour approved notary public education course satisfies the requirement for a three-hour refresher course. A six-hour approved education course always satisfies the education requirement, regardless if you are a new applicant or applying for reappointment.

Q. What are the requirements for applicants to be eligible to take an approved three-hour refresher education course?

A. A notary public who has previously completed an approved six-hour notary public education course is eligible to take an approved three-hour refresher course if the notary public has taken the notary public exam and submitted the application at the exam site prior to the expiration date of the current commission.

Q. I applied for reappointment prior to the expiration date of my current notary public commission and took an approved three-hour notary public education course, but I failed the notary public exam. What do I do now?

A. If you can take the exam again prior to the expiration date of your current commission, the proof of completion certificate from the three-hour course would still be valid. Attach the proof of completion certificate to your application, along with a 2" x 2" color passport photo of yourself and a check for twenty dollars ($20) when you go to the exam site. However, if your commission expires prior to retaking the exam, the three-hour course no longer meets the education requirements and you will need to take an approved six-hour course. You will need to attach the proof of completion certificate from the approved six-hour notary public education course to the application, along with a 2" x 2" color passport photo of yourself and a check for twenty dollars ($20).

Q. I did not file my oath and bond on time. What do I do?

A. If you are a new applicant and took an approved six-hour notary public education course, you must attach a current proof of completion certificate to a new application, along with a 2" x 2" color passport photo of yourself and a check for twenty dollars ($20). You will also need to have your fingerprints retaken at a Live Scan site.

If you are a notary public seeking reappointment and took an approved three-hour notary public refresher education course, you will still need to take an approved six-hour course. The three-hour course no longer meets the education requirements because your current commission has expired. You will need to attach the proof of completion certificate for the six-hour course to a new application, along with a 2" x 2" color passport photo of yourself and a check for twenty dollars ($20).You will also need to have your fingerprints retaken at a Live Scan site.

If you are a notary public seeking reappointment and took an approved six-hour education course, you must attach a current proof of completion certificate to a new application, along with a 2" x 2" color passport photo of yourself and a check for twenty dollars ($20). You will also need to have your fingerprints retaken at a Live Scan site.

Q. Where can I get a Live Scan fingerprint form?

A. The Live Scan fingerprint form is available on the Secretary of State's website or upon request from the Secretary of State's office.

Q. I have completed an approved course of study and taken the exam, but my current commission doesn't expire for another four months. When will I receive my new

commission?

A. Your notary public commission for reappointment will be issued 30 days prior to the expiration date of your current commission if you have complied with all the requirements to become a notary public.

Q. I have changed my business, mailing or home address. What do I do?

A. Send the Secretary of State a letter or a change of address form by certified mail or any other means of physical delivery that provides a receipt within 30 days of the change. (Government Code section 8213.5)

Q. I have changed my business from one county to another. What do I do?

A. Your commission allows you to notarize throughout the State of California, regardless of where your oath and bond are on file. If the location of your business has changed, you are required to send the Secretary of State an address change by certified mail or any other means of physical delivery that provides a receipt within 30 days of the change. If the address change is for your business, please include the business name in your notification. If the address change includes a change of county, you may choose to file a new oath of office and bond in the county to which your business has moved, however, a county transfer is not required. To file a county change, you must request an oath of office form from the Secretary of State. The oath will have the name of your original county; however, you must take and file your oath of office in the new county, checking the county transfer box at the bottom of the oath form. You also must take a new bond or a duplicate of the original bond and file it together with your oath of office in the new county. A certificate of authorization to manufacture a notary public seal will be sent to you once the Secretary of State has received and processed your oath of office filed in the new county. Your stamp must reflect the county where your most recent oath and bond are filed. (Government Code sections 8213 and 8213.5)

Q. Am I required to see the person sign the document at the time I perform the notarization?

A. It depends on the document being notarized. When preparing a jurat, the person requesting the jurat must appear before you, take an oath, and sign the document in your presence. When preparing a certificate of acknowledgment, the document can be executed before the person brings it to you for notarization. In an acknowledgment, the signer must personally appear before you and acknowledge that the signer executed the document, not that the signer executed the document in your presence. For both a jurat and an acknowledgment, the notary public must certify to the identity of the signer. (Civil Code section 1189 and Government Code section 8202)

Q. I lost my stamp or journal. What do I do?

A. Send a letter immediately by certified mail or any other means of physical delivery that provides a receipt to the Secretary of State explaining what happened and, if applicable, a photocopy of a police report. Upon written request, the Secretary of State will send an authorization so you can have a new stamp made. (Government Code sections 8206 and 8207.3(e))

Q. I have changed my name. What do I do?

A. Send a completed name change form to the Secretary of State. Once approved, you will be issued an amended commission that reflects your new name. Next, you will need to file a new oath of office and an amendment to your bond with the county clerk within 30 days from the date the amended commission was issued in order for the name change to take effect. Within 30 days of the fling, you must obtain a new seal that reflects the new name. Once the amended oath and bond are filed, you may no longer use the commission, including the stamp, that was issued in your previous name. If you fail to file your amended oath and bond within the 30-day time limit, the name change will become void and your commission will revert back to the previous name and you will be required to submit another name change application. (Government Code sections 8213 and 8213.6)

Q. I need to request a new certificate of authorization to have a new stamp made. Is there a fee?

A. No. However, you must send the Secretary of State a written request for a certificate of authorization. (Government Code section 8207.3(e))

Q. How do I resign my commission?

A. If you want to resign your commission, send a letter of resignation to the Secretary of State's office; within 30 days deliver all of your notarial journals, records and papers to the county clerk in which your current oath of office is on file; and destroy your seal. (Government Code section 8209)

Q. What parts of my notary public application are public information?

A. Under Government Code section 8201.5, only your name and address may be provided to the general public. All other information provided on a notary public application is confidential.

SUMMARY

This section is self-explanatory and won't be covered with a summary or a true false question.

GOVERNMENT CODE

§ 8200. Appointment and commission; number; jurisdiction

The Secretary of State may appoint and commission notaries public in such number as the Secretary of State deems necessary for the public convenience. Notaries public may act as such notaries in any part of this state.

SUMMARY

The Secretary of State may appoint and issue any number of notary public commissions it sees fit to maintain convenient access for the public. A notary public may therefore perform notarial acts anywhere in the state.

TRUE OR FALSE?

29.   The number of notaries public commissioned by the Secretary of State is based on convenience for the public.

✓ Answer key on Page 222

§ 8201. Qualifications to be a notary public; proof of course completion; reappointment

(a).   Every person appointed as notary public shall meet all of the following requirements:
(1)   Be at the time of appointment a legal resident of this state, except as otherwise provided in Section 8203.1.
(2)   Be not less than 18 years of age.
(3)   For appointments made on or after July 1, 2005, have satisfactorily completed a six-hour course of study approved by the Secretary of State pursuant to Section 8201.2 concerning the functions and duties of a notary public.
(4)   Have satisfactorily completed a written examination prescribed by the Secretary of State to determine the fitness of the person to exercise the functions and duties of the office of notary public. All questions shall be based on the law of this state as set forth in the booklet of the laws of California relating to notaries public distributed by the Secretary of State.
(b).   (1) Commencing July 1, 2005, each applicant for notary public shall provide

satisfactory proof that he or she has completed the course of study required pursuant to paragraph (3) of subdivision (a) prior to approval of his or her appointment as a notary public by the Secretary of State.

(2)   Commencing July 1, 2005, an applicant for notary public who holds a California notary public commission, and who has satisfactorily completed the six-hour course of study required pursuant to paragraph (1) at least one time, shall provide satisfactory proof when applying for reappointment as a notary public that he or she has satisfactorily completed a three-hour refresher course of study prior to reappointment as a notary public by the Secretary of State.

SUMMARY

A notary public must:

- Be a legal resident of California; and
- Be at least 18 years of age; and
- Have completed a Secretary of State-approved six-hour study course and provide proof to the Secretary of State if applying for the first time or applying after their prior commission has expired; or
- Have completed a Secretary of State-approved three-hour refresher course and provide proof to the Secretary of State if the renewal applicant's commission is current and he/she has completed an approved six-hour study course at least once before; and
- Pass a Secretary of State-approved written exam.

TRUE OR FALSE?

30.   If a renewal applicant has previously completed a six-hour study course in the past, he/she only needs to take a three-hour refresher course, even if their commission has expired.

✓ Answer key on Page 222

§ 8201.1. Additional qualifications; determination; identification; fingerprints

(a). Prior to granting an appointment as a notary public, the Secretary of State shall determine that the applicant possesses the required honesty, credibility, truthfulness, and integrity to fulfill the responsibilities of the position. To assist in determining the identity of the applicant and whether the applicant has been convicted of a disqualifying crime specified in subdivision (b) of Section 8214.1, the Secretary of State shall require that applicants be fingerprinted.

(b). Applicants shall submit to the Department of Justice fingerprint images and related information required by the department for the purpose of obtaining information as to the existence and content of a record of state and federal convictions and arrests and information as to the existence and content of a record of state and federal arrests for which the department establishes that the person is free on bail, or on his or her recognizance, pending trial or appeal.

(c). The department shall forward the fingerprint images and related information received pursuant to subdivision (a) to the Federal Bureau of Investigation and request a federal summary of criminal information.

(d). The department shall review the information returned from the Federal Bureau of Investigation and compile and disseminate a response to the Secretary of State pursuant to paragraph (1) of subdivision (p) of Section 11105 of the Penal Code.

(e). The Secretary of State shall request from the department subsequent arrest notification service, pursuant to Section 11105.2 of the Penal Code, for each person who submitted information pursuant to subdivision (a).The department shall charge a fee sufficient to cover the cost of processing the requests described in this section.

SUMMARY

For appointment as a notary public, the applicant must be honest, credible, and truthful enough to perform notarial responsibilities, as determined by the Secretary of State. Applicants shall submit their fingerprints and information to the Department of Justice for review, examination, which will be forwarded to the FBI. Both agencies will search for criminal records of the applicant, if any. The Department of Justice will provide the Secretary of State with its response after the search is complete and the Secretary of State will request notification from the Department of any future arrests of the applicant. A fee will be charged by the Secretary of State to cover the expense of these investigations.

TRUE OR FALSE?

31. An applicant's fingerprints and accompanying information will be used to prove the applicant's identity and criminal history.

✓ Answer key on Page 222

§ 8201.2. Review of course of study for notary public; approval of

education course of study, violation of regulations; civil penalties

(a) The Secretary of State shall review the course of study proposed by any vendor to be offered pursuant to paragraph (3) of subdivision (a) and paragraph (2) of subdivision (b) of Section 8201. If the course of study includes all material that a person is expected to know to satisfactorily complete the written examination required pursuant to paragraph (4) of subdivision of Section 8201, the Secretary of State shall approve the course of study.

(b) (1) The Secretary of State shall, by regulation, prescribe an application form and adopt a certificate of approval for the notary public education course of study proposed by a vendor.

(2) The Secretary of State may also provide a notary public education course of study.

(c) The Secretary of State shall compile a list of all persons offering an approved course of study pursuant to subdivision (a) and shall provide the list with every booklet of the laws of California relating to notaries public distributed by the Secretary of State.

(d) (1) A person who provides notary public education and violates any of the regulations adopted by the Secretary of State for approved vendors is subject to a civil penalty not to exceed one thousand dollars ($1,000) for each violation and shall be required to pay restitution where appropriate.

(2) The local district attorney, city attorney, or the Attorney General may bring a civil action to recover the civil penalty prescribed pursuant to this subdivision. A public prosecutor shall inform the Secretary of State of any civil penalty imposed under this section.

SUMMARY

The Secretary of State reviews any notary public study course proposed by a vendor and will approve the course if it contains all the material an applicant must know to pass the exam. The Secretary of State shall have a specific application form and certificate of approval. The Secretary of State may also independently provide a notary public education study course. The Secretary of State shall provide a list of all approved course providers along with every Notary Public Handbook. Any study course provider violating the Secretary of State's regulations on study courses may be charged by a local district attorney, city attorney, or Attorney General with a civil penalty of $1,000.00 or less for each violation and pay restitution if appropriate.

TRUE OR FALSE?

32. A vendor can provide a notary public study course while waiting for the Secretary of State's approval.

✓ Answer key on Page 222

§ 8201.5. Application form; confidential nature; use of information

The Secretary of State shall require an applicant for appointment and commission as a notary public to complete an application form and submit a photograph of their person as prescribed by the Secretary of State. Information on this form filed by an applicant with the Secretary of State, except for his or her name and address, is confidential and no individual record shall be divulged by an official or employee having access to it to any person other than the applicant, his or her authorized representative, or an employee or officer of the federal government, the state government, or a local agency, as defined in subdivision (b) of Section 6252 of the Government Code, acting in his or her official capacity. That information shall be used by the Secretary of State for the sole purpose of carrying out the duties of this chapter.

SUMMARY

The Secretary of State requires every applicant to submit a completed application and photograph. All information on the application is confidential, except the applicant's name and address. Anyone who has access to the filed application are prohibited from disclosing the applicant's confidential information, except to the applicant; anyone authorized by the applicant; or to any state, federal, or local government officer in an official capacity. The application shall only be used by the Secretary of State for the purpose of appointment and commission as a notary public.

TRUE OR FALSE?

33.   An applicant's fingerprints and accompanying information will be used to prove the applicant's identity and criminal history.

✓ Answer key on Page 222

§ 8202. Execution of jurat; administration of oath or affirmation to affiant; attachment to affidavit

(a) When executing a jurat, a notary shall administer an oath or affirmation to the affiant and shall determine, from satisfactory evidence as described in Section 1185 of the Civil Code, that the affiant is the person executing the document. The affiant shall sign the document in the presence of the notary.

(b) To any affidavit subscribed and sworn to before a notary, there shall be attached a jurat that includes a notice at the top, in an enclosed box, stating: "A notary public or other officer completing this certificate verifies only the identity of the individual who signed the document to which this certificate is attached, and not the truthfulness, accuracy, or validity of that document." This notice shall be legible.

(c) The physical format of the boxed notice at the top of the jurat required pursuant to subdivision (d) is an example, for purposes of illustration and not limitation, of the physical format of a boxed notice fulfilling the requirements of subdivision (b).

(d) A jurat executed pursuant to this section shall be in the following form:

> A notary public or other officer completing this
> certificate verifies only the identity of the
> individual who signed the document to which this
> certificate is attached, and not the truthfulness,
> accuracy, or validity of that document.

State of California
County of _____
Subscribed and sworn to (or affirmed) before me on this _____ day of _____, 20___, by _____, proved to me on the basis of satisfactory evidence to be the person(s) who appeared before me.

    Seal _____
    Signature _____

SUMMARY

A notary public shall administer an oath or affirmation to an affiant when executing a jurat. The notary shall determine the affiant's identity by satisfactory evidence as defined by Civil Code section 1185, and the affiant must sign the document in the presence of the notary. Any affidavit subscribed and sworn to before a notary public must have a jurat which includes a legible notice enclosed in a box at the top of the jurat, stating "A notary public or other officer completing this certificate verifies only the identity of the individual who signed the document to which this certificate is attached, and not the truthfulness, accuracy, or validity of that document." Reference the form found in the official section above for an example of a proper jurat defined in this paragraph.

TRUE OR FALSE?

34.   A proper jurat must have a legible notice that the notary public is only verifying the identity and signature of the person but there's no specific language for it and it doesn't have to be in a box.

✓ Answer key on Page 222

§ 8202.5. State, county and school district employees; certificates; expenses

The Secretary of State may appoint and commission the number of state, city, county, and public school district employees as notaries public to act for and on behalf of the governmental entity for which appointed which the Secretary of State deems proper. Whenever a notary is appointed and commissioned, a duly authorized representative of the employing governmental entity shall execute a certificate that the appointment is made for the purposes of the employing governmental entity, and whenever the certificate is filed with any state or county officer, no fees shall be charged by the officer for the filing or issuance of any document in connection with the appointment.
The state or any city, county, or school district for which the notary public is appointed and commissioned pursuant to this section may pay from any funds available for its support the premiums on any bond and the cost of any stamps, seals, or other supplies required in connection with the appointment, commission, or performance of the duties of the notary public.

Any fees collected or obtained by any notary public whose documents have been filed without charge and for whom bond premiums have been paid by the employer of the notary public shall be remitted by the notary public to the employing agency which shall deposit the funds to the credit of the fund from which the salary of the notary public is paid.

SUMMARY

The Secretary of State may appoint and commission a government employee as a notary public to provide notary services for the government employer. If necessary, the government employer will sign and file a certificate regarding the appointment at no cost. The employer must pay all expenses related to the notary's appointment, commission, and notarial services for their government employer. The notary public must also remit any notary fees collected to the government employer, who shall then deposit those funds into the payroll account from which the notary public's wages are paid.

TRUE OR FALSE?

35.   An employee of a government agency who is specifically appointed and commissioned to provide notary services for that agency must relinquish their seal, stamp, and notary journal(s) to the government agency upon terminating their employment because the agency paid for all expenses related to the notary's commission, bond, and supplies.

✓ Answer key on Page 222

§ 8202.7. Private employers; agreement to pay premium on bonds and costs of supplies; remission of fees to employer

A private employer, pursuant to an agreement with an employee who is a notary public, may pay the premiums on any bond and the cost of any stamps, seals, or other supplies required in connection with the appointment, commission, or performance of the duties of such notary public. Such agreement may also provide for the remission of fees collected by such notary public to the employer, in which case any fees collected or obtained by such notary public while such agreement is in effect shall be remitted by such notary public to the employer which shall deposit such funds to the credit of the fund from which the compensation of the notary public is paid.

SUMMARY

A notary public and their private employer may mutually agree to allow the employer to pay all expenses related to the notary's appointment, commission, and materials to provide notarial services to the employer. The agreement may also require the notary to remit all notary fees collected to the employer who must then deposit the funds into the account from which the notary public's wages are paid.

TRUE OR FALSE?

36.   The private employer of a notary public is required to pay all the notary public's expenses for appointment, commission, and performance of notary services for the private employer.

✓ Answer key on Page 222

§ 8202.8. Private employers; limitation on provision of notarial services

Notwithstanding any other provision of law, a private employer of a notary public who has entered into an agreement with his or her employee pursuant to Section 8202.7 may limit, during the employee's ordinary course of employment, the providing of notarial services by the employee solely to transactions directly associated with the business purposes of the employer.

SUMMARY

A private employer who has entered into an agreement with its notary public employee as described in Section 8202.7 may restrict that employee from providing notarial services for any person or entity other than the employer for so long as the notary public is employed with the private employer.

TRUE OR FALSE?

37.   If a private employer has paid for all expenses related to a notary public employee's appointment, commission, and materials, the employer can restrict the notary public from performing notarial services for anyone else for the duration of the notary public's commission.

✓ Answer key on Page 222

§ 8203.1. Military and naval reservations; appointment and commission of notaries; qualifications

The Secretary of State may appoint and commission notaries public for the military and naval reservations of the Army, Navy, Coast Guard, Air Force, and Marine Corps of the United States, wherever located in the state; provided, however, that the appointee shall be a citizen of the United States, not less than 18 years of age, and must meet the requirements set forth in paragraphs (3) and (4) of subdivision (a) of Section 8201.

SUMMARY

The Secretary of State may appoint and commission a notary public to provide notary services on any United States military/naval reservation anywhere in the state if the appointee is a citizen of the United States, at least 18 years of age, has completed an approved notary public training course, and has passed the written exam.

TRUE OR FALSE?

38. A person can be appointed as a notary public on any military/naval reservation located anywhere in the United States.

✓ Answer key on Page 222

§ 8203.2. Military and naval reservations, recommendation of commanding officer; jurisdiction of notary

Such notaries public shall be appointed only upon the recommendation of the commanding officer of the reservation in which they are to act, and they shall be authorized to act only within the boundaries of this reservation.

SUMMARY

No one may be appointed and commissioned as a notary public on a military/naval reservation unless the commanding officer of that military/naval reservation has specifically recommended the appointee and the appointee is only authorized to act within the boundaries of the specific military/naval reservation.

TRUE OR FALSE?

39. If a commanding officer recommends a person for appointment as a notary public on the commanding officer's military/naval reservation, that person shall be automatically appointed as a notary public by the Secretary of State but may only perform notarial acts on that reservation.

✓ Answer key on Page 222

§ 8203.3. Military and naval reservations, qualifications of notaries

In addition to the qualifications established in Section 8203.1, appointments will be made only from among those persons who are federal civil service employees at the reservation in which they will act as notaries public.

SUMMARY

Appointments will only be made for federal civil service employees who work at the military/naval reservation where they will perform notary services. They must also be a citizen of the United States, at least 18 years of age, complete an approved notary public training course, and pass the written exam.

TRUE OR FALSE?

40. A person may only be appointed as a notary public on a military/naval reservation if they (1) are also a federal civil service employee on that reservation; and (2) comply with all of the usual requirements for appointment and they are also a federal civil service employee on the reservation where they will be performing notarial acts.

✓ Answer key on Page 222

§ 8203.4. Military and naval reservations; term of office; termination; resignation

The term of office shall be as set forth in Section 8204, except that the appointment shall terminate if the person shall cease to be employed as a federal civil service employee at the reservation for which appointed. The commanding officer of the reservation shall notify the Secretary of State of termination of employment at the reservation for which appointed within 30 days of such termination. A notary public whose appointment terminates pursuant to this section will have such termination treated as a resignation.

SUMMARY

The term of office for a notary public employed on a military/naval reservation is four years unless the notary's employment on that military/naval reservation is terminated sooner. If the notary public's employment is terminated, their appointment is also immediately terminated and is treated as the notary's resignation of their commission. The commanding officer of the reservation must notify the Secretary of State of the notary's employment termination within 30 days.

TRUE OR FALSE?

41. A notary public appointed to a military/naval reservation where he/she is a federal civil service employee is allowed one four-year commission unless their employment ends

sooner, at which time their commission immediately terminates as well.

✓ Answer key on Page 222

§ 8203.5. Military and naval reservations, jurat

In addition to the name of the State, the jurat shall also contain the name of the reservation in which the instrument is executed.

SUMMARY

For a jurat to be completed and signed on a military/naval reservation, the name of the reservation must be included with the name of the State.

§ 8203.6. Military and naval reservations, fees

No fees shall be collected by such notaries public for service rendered within the reservation in the capacity of a notary public.

SUMMARY

The notary public shall not collect fees for notarial acts performed within the military reservation.

§ 8204. Term of office

The term of office of a notary public is for four years commencing with the date specified in the commission.

SUMMARY

A notary public's term of office is four years starting from the date of the commission.

§ 8204.1. Cancellation of Commission; failure to pay; notice

The Secretary of State may cancel the commission of a notary public if a check or other remittance accepted as payment for the examination, application, commission, and fingerprint fee is not paid upon presentation to the financial institution upon which the check or other remittance was drawn. Upon receiving written notification that the item presented for payment has not been honored for payment, the Secretary of State shall first give a written notice of the applicability of this section to the notary public or the person submitting the instrument. Thereafter, if the amount is not paid by a cashier's check or the equivalent, the Secretary of State shall give a second written notice of cancellation and the cancellation shall thereupon be effective. This second notice shall be given at least 20 days after the first notice, and no more than 90 days after the commencement date of the commission.

SUMMARY

The Secretary of State may cancel a notary public's commission if any payment made by the notary public is returned unpaid. The notary will receive a first written notice that their commission may be canceled for non-payment. If the notary does not immediately pay the required amount via cashier's check or equivalent, the notary will receive a second written notice of cancellation 20 days after the first notice, but no more than 90 days from the date of the commission. The second written notice will inform the notary public that their commission is canceled effective immediately.

TRUE OR FALSE?

42.   A notary public whose payment to the Secretary of State has been returned may instruct the Secretary of State's office to resubmit the payment to the bank.

✓ Answer key on Page 222

§ 8205. Duties

(a) It is the duty of a notary public, when requested:
(1) To demand acceptance and payment of foreign and inland bills of exchange, or promissory notes, to protest them for nonacceptance and nonpayment, and, with regard only to the nonacceptance or nonpayment of bills and notes, to exercise any other powers and duties that by the law of nations and according to commercial usages, or by the laws of any other state, government, or country, may be performed by a notary. This paragraph applies only to a notary public employed by a financial institution, during the course and scope of the notary's employment with the financial institution.
(2) To take the acknowledgment or proof of advance health care directives, powers of attorney, mortgages, deeds, grants, transfers, and other instruments of writing executed by any person, and to give a certificate of that proof or acknowledgment, endorsed on or attached to the instrument. The certificate shall be signed by the notary public in the

notary public's own handwriting. A notary public may not accept any acknowledgment or proof of any instrument that is incomplete.

(3) To take depositions and affidavits, and administer oaths and affirmations, in all matters incident to the duties of the office, or to be used before any court, judge, officer, or board. Any deposition, affidavit, oath, or affirmation shall be signed by the notary public in the notary public's own handwriting.

(4) To certify copies of powers of attorney under Section 4307 of the Probate Code. The certification shall be signed by the notary public in the notary public's own handwriting.

(b) It shall further be the duty of a notary public, upon written request:

(1) To furnish to the Secretary of State certified copies of the notary's journal.

(2) To respond within 30 days of receiving written requests sent by certified mail or any other means of physical delivery that provides a receipt from the Secretary of State's office for information relating to official acts performed by the notary.

SUMMARY

If requested, a notary public must perform certain duties specific to financial institutions only if and while the notary is employed by the financial institution requesting said duties.

If requested, a notary public has a duty to witness the acknowledgment of any advance health care directives, powers of attorney, mortgages, deeds, grants, transfers, and other instruments as long as they are complete. The notary must provide a certificate of acknowledgment, either endorsed on the instrument or attached to it.

To take depositions and affidavits, and administer oaths and affirmations, then sign them in the notary public's own handwriting.

To certify copies of powers of attorney. The certification shall be signed by the notary public in the notary public's own handwriting.

To provide the Secretary of State certified copies of the notary's journal.

To respond within 30 days to any written request for information relating to official acts performed by the notary and sent by any delivery method which provides a receipt.

TRUE OR FALSE?

43.   A notary public has a duty to certify a copy of a copy of a power of attorney.

✓ Answer key on Page 222

§ 8206. Sequential journal; contents; thumbprint; loss of journal; copies of pages; exclusive property of notary public; limitations on surrender

(a) (1) A notary public shall keep one active sequential journal at a time, of all official acts performed as a notary public. The journal shall be kept in a locked and secured area, under the direct and exclusive control of the notary. Failure to secure the journal shall be cause for the Secretary of State to take administrative action against the commission held by the notary public pursuant to Section 8214.1.

(2) The journal shall be in addition to, and apart from, any copies of notarized documents that may be in the possession of the notary public and shall include all of the following:

(A) Date, time, and type of each official act.

(B) Character of every instrument sworn to, affirmed, acknowledged, or proved before the notary.

(C) The signature of each person whose signature is being notarized.

(D) A statement as to whether the identity of a person making an acknowledgment or taking an oath or affirmation was based on satisfactory evidence. If identity was established by satisfactory evidence pursuant to Section 1185 of the Civil Code, the journal shall contain the signature of the credible witness swearing or affirming to the identity of the individual or the type of identifying document, the governmental agency issuing the document, the serial or identifying number of the document, and the date of issue or expiration of the document.

(E) If the identity of the person making the acknowledgment or taking the oath or affirmation was established by the oaths or affirmations of two credible witnesses whose identities are proven to the notary public by presentation of any document satisfying the requirements of paragraph (3) or (4) of subdivision (b) of Section 1185 of the Civil Code, the notary public shall record in the journal the type of documents identifying the witnesses, the identifying numbers on the documents identifying the witnesses, and the dates of issuance or expiration of the documents identifying the witnesses.

(F) The fee charged for the notarial service.

(G) If the document to be notarized is a deed, quitclaim deed, deed of trust, or other document affecting real property, or a power of attorney document, the notary public shall require the party signing the document to place his or her right thumbprint in the journal. If the right thumbprint is not available, then the notary shall have the party use his or her left thumb, or any available finger and shall so indicate in the journal. If the party signing the document is physically unable to provide a thumbprint or fingerprint, the notary shall so indicate in the journal and shall also provide an explanation of that physical condition. This paragraph shall not apply to a trustee's deed resulting from a decree of foreclosure or a nonjudicial foreclosure pursuant to Section 2924 of the Civil Code, nor to a deed of reconveyance.

(b) If a sequential journal of official acts performed by a notary public is stolen, lost, misplaced, destroyed, damaged, or otherwise rendered unusable as a record of notarial acts and information, the notary public shall immediately notify the Secretary of State by certified or registered mail or any other means of physical delivery that provides a receipt. The notification shall include the period of the journal entries, the notary public commission number, and the expiration date of the commission, and when applicable, a photocopy of any police report that specifies the theft of the sequential journal of official acts.

(c) Upon written request of any member of the public, which request shall include the name of the parties, the type of document, and the month and year in which notarized, the notary shall supply a photostatic copy of the line item representing the requested transaction at a cost of not more than thirty cents ($0.30) per page.

(d) The journal of notarial acts of a notary public is the exclusive property of that notary public and shall not be surrendered to an employer upon termination of employment, whether or not the employer paid for the journal, or at any other time. The notary public shall not surrender the journal to any other person, except the county clerk, pursuant to Section 8209, or immediately, or if the journal is not present then as soon as possible, upon request to a peace officer investigating a criminal offense who has reasonable suspicion to believe the journal contains evidence of a criminal offense, as defined in Sections 830.1, 830.2, and 830.3 of the Penal Code, acting in his or her official capacity and within his or her authority. If the peace officer seizes the notary journal, he or she must have probable cause as required by the laws of this state and the United States. A peace officer or law enforcement agency that seizes a notary journal shall notify the Secretary of State by facsimile within 24 hours, or as soon as possible thereafter, of the name of the notary public whose journal has been seized. The notary public shall obtain a receipt for the journal and shall notify the Secretary of State by certified mail any other means of physical delivery that provides a receipt within 10 days that the journal was relinquished to a peace officer. The notification shall include the period of the journal entries, the commission number of the notary public, the expiration date of the commission, and a photocopy of the receipt. The notary public shall obtain a new sequential journal. If the journal relinquished to a peace officer is returned to the notary public and a new journal has been obtained, the notary public shall make no new entries in the returned journal. A notary public who is an employee shall permit inspection and copying of journal transactions by a duly designated auditor or agent of the notary public's employer, provided that the inspection and copying is done in the presence of the notary public and the transactions are directly associated with the business purposes of the employer. The notary public, upon the request of the employer, shall regularly provide copies of all transactions that are directly associated with the business purposes of the employer, but shall not be required to provide copies of any transaction that is unrelated to the employer's business. Confidentiality and safekeeping of any copies of the journal provided to the employer shall be the responsibility of that employer.

(e) The notary public shall provide the journal for examination and copying in the presence of the notary public upon receipt of a subpoena duces tecum or a court order and shall certify those copies if requested.

(f) Any applicable requirements of, or exceptions to, state and federal law shall apply to a peace officer engaged in the search or seizure of a sequential journal.

SUMMARY

A notary public must only keep one active sequentially numbered journal at a time in a place where it is locked and secured under the direct and sole control of the notary public. If the notary does not make sure the journal is locked and secured, the notary public may be administratively punished.

The notary journal must contain: the date, time, and type of each official act; the signer's signature; whether or not the signer's identity was based upon satisfactory evidence; if the signer's identity was based upon the oaths of two credible witnesses, all details about the witnesses and identity documents; the fee charged; and the signer's thumbprint if the instrument involves real estate or a power of attorney.

If a notary public's journal is stolen, lost, misplaced, damaged, or otherwise unusable, the notary must immediately notify the Secretary of State by a delivery method which provides a receipt, along with a copy of any police report made regarding the theft of the journal, if applicable. The notary must provide the following information: time period of entries in the journal; the notary's commission number; and expiration date of the notary's commission.

If a notary public receives a written request from any member of the public with the name of the parties; document type; and date of notarization, the notary must provide a copy of the specific line in their journal or written acknowledgment that no such information exists. The notary may not charge more than $0.30 per page to provide the response.

A notary public must never surrender their notary journal(s) to anyone other than the county clerk or to law enforcement personnel if the journal is believed to be evidence of a crime, but only with probable cause and pursuant to the state and federal laws concerning search and seizure. The notary must obtain a receipt for the notary journal upon presenting it to the appropriate party and notify the Secretary of State by verifiable means within 10 days of relinquishing it to law enforcement. A notary public must allow copying of their journal by the notary's employer as long as the notary is present at all times during the examination and copying AND copying is strictly limited to transactions pertain only to the employer's business operations. Any other unrelated notarizations shall remain confidential.

A notary public must provide their journal for examination and copying in the notary public's presence in response to a subpoena duces tecum or court order. The notary shall also certify the copies if requested.

TRUE OR FALSE?

44.   A notary public may allow an employer to copy the notary journal at an off-site copy center as long as it is their current employer, and the employer returns the journal to the notary within a reasonable amount of time.

✓ Answer key on Page 222

§ 8206.5. Notaries; supplying photostatic copies on request; defending position in a disciplinary proceeding

Upon receiving a request for a copy of a transaction pursuant to subdivision (c) of Section 8206, the notary shall respond to the request within 15 business days after receipt of the request and either supply the photostatic copy requested or acknowledge that no such line item exists. In a disciplinary proceeding for noncompliance with subdivision (c) of Section 8206 or this section, a notary may defend his or her delayed action on the basis of unavoidable, exigent business or personal circumstances.

SUMMARY

A notary public has 15 business days to respond to a written request for a copy of a transaction from their notary journal. The notary will respond by providing a photocopy of the specific line from the notary public's journal OR by providing a written acknowledgment that no such line item exists. If a notary doesn't comply and a disciplinary proceeding is held, the notary has a valid defense for their delayed action due to unavoidable business or personal circumstances.

TRUE OR FALSE?

45.   A notary public must provide a copy of a transaction in their notary journal or a written acknowledgment that no such transaction exists within 15 days of a written request.

✓ Answer key on Page 222

§ 8207. Seal

A notary public shall provide and keep an official seal, which shall clearly show, when embossed, stamped, impressed or affixed to a document, the name of the notary, the State

Seal, the words "Notary Public," and the name of the county wherein the bond and oath of office are filed, and the date the notary public's commission expires. The seal of every notary public commissioned on or after January 1, 1992, shall contain the sequential identification number assigned to the notary and the sequential identification number assigned to the manufacturer or vendor. The notary public shall authenticate with the official seal all official acts. A notary public shall not use the official notarial seal except for the purpose of carrying out the duties and responsibilities as set forth in this chapter. A notary public shall not use the title "notary public" except for the purpose of rendering notarial service.

The seal of every notary public shall be affixed by a seal press or stamp that will print or emboss a seal which legibly reproduces under photographic methods the required elements of the seal. The seal may be circular not over two inches in diameter, or may be a rectangular form of not more than one inch in width by two and one-half inches in length, with a serrated or milled edged border, and shall contain the information required by this section.

The seal shall be kept in a locked and secured area, under the direct and exclusive control of the notary. Failure to secure the seal shall be cause for the Secretary of State to take administrative action against the commission held by the notary public pursuant to Section 8214.1.

The official seal of a notary public is the exclusive property of that notary public and shall not be surrendered to an employer upon the termination of employment, whether or not the employer paid for the seal, or to any other person. The notary, or his or her representative, shall destroy or deface the seal upon termination, resignation, or revocation of the notary's commission.

This section shall become operative on January 1, 1992.

SUMMARY

A notary public shall keep a seal which clearly shows the notary's name, the state seal, the words "Notary Public", and the name of the county where the notary's bond and oath are filed. A sequential number identifying the notary and one identifying the vendor shall also be included on the seal. The seal must be clear and dark enough to photocopy legibly, and not be any larger than 2" in diameter (circular seal) or no larger than 1" x 2.5" (rectangular seal) with a milled edged border.

The notary public must keep the seal in a locked and secured area under their sole access and control. Failure to do so may result in disciplinary action against the notary public. The notary public is the only owner of their official seal and must never relinquish the seal to anyone, including an employer or former employer. The notary public must destroy their official seal once their commission is no longer active for any reason.

TRUE OR FALSE?

46.   Once a notary public's commission is terminated or expired, the notary can just toss their seal in the trash to dispose of it.

✓ Answer key on Page 222

§ 8207.1. Identification number

The Secretary of State shall assign a sequential identification number to each notary which shall appear on the notary commission.

SUMMARY

Each notary public shall have an identification number appearing on their commission, which is assigned by the Secretary of State in consecutive order.

TRUE OR FALSE?

47.   Every notary public is assigned an identification number by the Secretary of State which is alphabetically based upon the notary's initials.

✓ Answer key on Page 222

§ 8207.2. Manufacture, duplication, and sale of seal or stamp; procedures and guidelines for issuance of seals; certificate of authorization

(a) No notary seal or press stamp shall be manufactured, duplicated, sold, or offered for sale unless authorized by the Secretary of State.
(b) The Secretary of State shall develop and implement procedures and guidelines for the issuance of notary seals on or before January 1, 1992.
(c) The Secretary of State shall issue a permit with a sequential identification number to each manufacturer or vendor authorized to issue notary seals. The Secretary of State may establish a fee for the issuance of the permit which shall not exceed the actual costs of issuing the permit.
(d) The Secretary of State shall develop a certificate of authorization to purchase a notary

stamp from an authorized vendor.

(e) The certificate of authorization shall be designed to prevent forgeries and shall contain a sequential identification number.

(f) This section shall become operative on January 1, 1992.

SUMMARY

No notary seal or stamp may be made, duplicated, sold, or even offered for sale without the authorization of the Secretary of State. The Secretary of State is required to develop and implement a system of rules and guidelines for all vendors who make and sell notary seals. Authorized vendors must have a consecutively numbered permit issued by the Secretary of State for a fee not to exceed the actual cost of issuing the permit. The Secretary of State must also develop and issue a consecutively numbered certificate of authorization which must be presented to an authorized vendor in order purchase a notary seal. The certificate of authorization must be designed with features to prevent forgery.

TRUE OR FALSE?

48.   A vendor is not authorized to manufacture and sell a notary seal until the vendor possesses a valid, consecutively numbered permit from the Secretary of State.

✓ Answer key on Page 222

§ 8207.3. Certificate of authorization; authorization to provide seal; lost, misplaced, damaged or otherwise unworkable seal

(a) The Secretary of State shall issue certificates of authorization with which a notary public can obtain an official notary seal.

(b) A vendor or manufacturer is authorized to provide a notary with an official seal only upon presentation by the notary public of a certificate of authorization.

(c) A vendor of official seals shall note the receipt of certificates of authorization and sequential identification numbers of certificates presented by a notary public upon a certificate of authorization.

(d) A copy of a certificate of authorization shall be retained by a vendor and the original, which shall contain a sample impression of the seal issued to the notary public, shall be submitted to the Secretary of State for verification and recordkeeping. The Secretary of State shall develop guidelines for submitting certificates of authorization by vendors.

(e) Any notary whose official seal is lost, misplaced, destroyed, broken, damaged, or is rendered otherwise unworkable shall immediately mail or deliver written notice of that fact to the Secretary of State. The Secretary of State, within five working days after receipt of the notice, if requested by a notary, shall issue a certificate of authorization which a notary may use to obtain a replacement seal.

(f) This section shall become operative on January 1, 1992.

SUMMARY

The Secretary of State issues each notary public a certificate of authorization which is required for the purchase of a notary seal from an authorized vendor. The authorized vendor will not make or sell any notary seal without a valid certificate of authorization and must keep a record of all certificates of authorization and the identification numbers of each certificate received. The authorized vendor must keep a copy of the certificate of authorization for their records, stamp the original certificate of authorization with the manufactured seal and then submit the stamped original to the Secretary of State according to the established requirements and guidelines.

If a notary public loses their official seal or it is otherwise destroyed, damaged, or unusable, the notary public must mail or deliver written notice to the Secretary of State immediately. Within five days after the notice, the Secretary of State shall issue the notary public a certificate of authorization to obtain a replacement seal if the notary requests one.

TRUE OR FALSE?

49.   The authorized vendor of notary seals must maintain a separate record with a photocopy of each certificate of authorization he/she receives and the commission number of each certificate.

✓ Answer key on Page 222

§ 8207.4. Violations; penalties

Any person who willfully violates any part of Section 8207.1, 8207.2, 8207.3, or 8207.4 shall be subject to a civil penalty not to exceed one thousand five hundred dollars ($1,500) for each violation, which may be recovered in a civil action brought by the Attorney General or the district attorney or city attorney, or by a city prosecutor in any city and county.

The penalty provided by this section is not an exclusive remedy and does not affect any other relief or remedy provided by law.

This section shall become operative on January 1, 1992.

SUMMARY

Any person who deliberately violates any part of Section 8207.1, 8207.2, 8207.3, or 8207.4 can be punished with a civil penalty in an amount no greater than $1,500.00 for each violation. A separate civil action may be filed against the violator by any attorney for the state, county, or city to collect the penalty money from the violator. This is not the only legal recourse for the violation(s), and other disciplinary actions, such as lawsuits or fines, may be imposed on the violator as well.

TRUE OR FALSE?

50.   A person who violates the above-named Sections on purpose can be punished with a fine no greater than $1,500.00 for each violation in addition to other civil, collections and garnishment lawsuits which may be filed against the person.

✓ Answer key on Page 222

§ 8208. Protest of bill or note for nonacceptance or nonpayment

The protest of a notary public acting in the course and scope of employment by a financial institution, under his or her hand and official seal, of a bill of exchange or promissory note for nonacceptance or nonpayment, specifying any of the following is prima facie evidence of the facts recited therein:
   (a) The time and place of presentment.
   (b) The fact that presentment was made and the manner thereof.
   (c) The cause or reason for protesting the bill.
   (d) The demand made and the answer given, if any, or the fact that the drawee or acceptor could not be found.

SUMMARY

If a notary public—acting in the usual role of their job at a financial institution—protests a bill of exchange or promissory note for nonacceptance or nonpayment, the notary's mention of any of the following items becomes self-evident proof of the facts stated in the protest:
   (a) The time and place the instrument was presented.
   (b) Confirmation that the instrument was presented and the way it was presented.
   (c) The basis for protesting the instrument.

(d) The demand that was made and the answer received, or that the beneficiary of the instrument couldn't be found.

TRUE OR FALSE?

51.   If a notary public employed by a financial institution protests a promissory note and makes a note on the instrument stating the reason for protesting the promissory note, no other evidence is needed to consider the details in the protest to be true.

✓ Answer key on Page 222

§ 8209. Resignation, disqualification or removal of notary; records delivered to clerk; misdemeanor; death; destruction of records

(a) If any notary public resigns, is disqualified, removed from office, or allows his or her appointment to expire without obtaining reappointment within 30 days, all notarial records and papers shall be delivered within 30 days to the clerk of the county in which the notary public's current official oath of office is on file. If the notary public willfully fails or refuses to deliver all notarial records and papers to the county clerk within 30 days, the person is guilty of a misdemeanor and shall be personally liable for damages to any person injured by that action or inaction.
(b) In the case of the death of a notary public, the personal representative of the deceased shall promptly notify the Secretary of State of the death of the notary public and shall deliver all notarial records and papers of the deceased to the clerk of the county in which the notary public's official oath of office is on file.
(c) After 10 years from the date of deposit with the county clerk, if no request for, or reference to such records has been made, they may be destroyed upon order of court.

SUMMARY

When any notary public's appointment is terminated for any reason, all of their notary records and papers must be delivered within 30 days to the county clerk where the notary's oath is on file. If the notary public deliberately fails to do it, the notary public is guilty of a misdemeanor and will be personally liable for any damages to any person impacted by the notary's actions/inactions. If the notary public has passed away, the personal representative of the deceased must promptly notify the Secretary of State and deliver all notarial records and papers to the county clerk where the notary's oath of office is filed. After 10 years from the date of the records delivery to the county clerk, and if no request or reference to the records has been made, the records may be destroyed with a court order.

TRUE OR FALSE?

52.   If a notary public has passed away, the executor or personal representative of the notary's estate may destroy the notary seal and all records as long as they inform the county clerk where the notary public's oath and bond were filed.

✓ Answer key on Page 222

§ 8211. Fees

Fees charged by a notary public for the following services shall not exceed the fees prescribed by this section.
(a) For taking an acknowledgment or proof of a deed, or other instrument, to include the seal and the writing of the certificate, the sum of fifteen dollars ($15) for each signature taken.
(b) For administering an oath or affirmation to one person and executing the jurat, including the seal, the sum of fifteen dollars ($15).
(c) For all services rendered in connection with the taking of any deposition, the sum of thirty dollars ($30), and in addition thereto, the sum of seven dollars ($7) for administering the oath to the witness and the sum of seven dollars ($7) for the certificate to the deposition.
(d) No fee may be charged to notarize signatures on vote by mail ballot identification envelopes or other voting materials.
(e) For certifying a copy of a power of attorney under Section 4307 of the Probate Code the sum of fifteen dollars ($15).

In accordance with Section 6107, no fee may be charged to a United States military veteran for notarization of an application or a claim for a pension, allotment, allowance, compensation, insurance, or any other veteran's benefit.

SUMMARY

The maximum fee a notary public may charge for notarial acts is prescribed by this section, as follows:

Service	Description	Maximum Fee
Acknowledgments	Acknowledgment or proof of a deed or other instrument, to include the seal and the writing of the certificate	$15 for each signature
Oaths/Affirmations	Administering an oath or affirmation to one person	$15
Jurats	Taking a person's oath and executing the jurat, with seal	$15
Deposition Services	All services rendered in connection with taking a deposition: - Administering the oath to the witness. - Certificate to the deposition.	$30 $7 $7
Voting Materials	Notarize signatures on vote by mail ballot identification envelopes or other voting materials	$0
Powers of Attorney	Certifying a copy of a power of attorney under Probate Code section 4307	$15

A notary may not charge any fee for notarizing an application or a claim by a United States military veteran for pension, allotment, allowance, compensation, insurance, or any other veteran's benefits.

TRUE OR FALSE?

53.   A notary public may not charge more than the fees prescribed in this section, but may charge less or nothing at all.

✓ Answer key on Page 222

§ 8212. Bond; amount; form

Every person appointed a notary public shall execute an official bond in the sum of fifteen thousand dollars ($15,000). The bond shall be in the form of a bond executed by an admitted surety insurer and not a deposit in lieu of bond.

SUMMARY

Every notary public must sign a $15,000.00 official bond by an admitted surety insurer, not just a monetary deposit in place of a surety bond.

§ 8213. Bonds and oaths; filing; certificate; copy of oath as evidence; transfer to new county; name changes; fees

(a) No later than 30 days after the beginning of the term prescribed in the commission, every person appointed a notary public shall file an official bond and an oath of office in the office of the county clerk of the county within which the person maintains a principal place of business as shown in the application submitted to the Secretary of State, and the commission shall not take effect unless this is done within the 30-day period. A person appointed to be a notary public shall take and subscribe the oath of office either in the office of that county clerk or +before another notary public in that county. If the oath of office is taken and subscribed before the county clerk, the person appointed to be a notary public shall present an identification document meeting the requirements of subparagraph (A) or (B) of paragraph (3), or of subparagraph (A) or (E) or paragraph (4), of subdivision (b) of Section 1185 of the Civil Code to the county clerk as satisfactory evidence of identity. If the oath of office is taken and subscribed before a notary public, the oath and bond may be filed with the county clerk by certified mail or any other means of physical delivery that provides a receipt. Upon the filing of the oath and bond, the county clerk shall immediately transmit to the Secretary of State a certificate setting forth the fact of the filing and containing a copy of the official oath, personally signed by the notary public in the form set forth in the commission and shall immediately deliver the bond to the county recorder for recording. The county clerk shall retain the oath of office for one year following the expiration of the term of the commission for which the oath was taken, after which the oath may be destroyed or otherwise disposed of. The copy of the oath, personally signed by the notary public, on file with the Secretary of State may at any time be read in evidence with like effect as the original oath, without further proof.

(b) If a notary public transfers the principal place of business from one county to another, the notary public may file a new oath of office and bond, or a duplicate of the original bond with the county clerk to which the principal place of business was transferred. If the notary public elects to make a new filing, the notary public shall, within 30 days of the filing, obtain an official seal which shall include the name of the county to which the notary public has transferred. In a case where the notary public elects to make a new filing, the same filing and recording fees are applicable as in the case of the original filing and recording of the bond.

(c) If a notary public submits an application for a name change to the Secretary of State, the notary public shall, within 30 days from the date an amended commission is issued, file a new oath of office and an amendment to the bond with the county clerk in which the principal place of business is located. The amended commission with the name change shall not take effect unless the filing is completed within the 30-day period. The amended commission with the name change takes effect the date the oath and amendment to the bond is filed with the county clerk. If the principal place of business address was changed in the application for name change, either a new or duplicate of the original bond shall be filed with the county clerk with the amendment to the bond. The notary public shall, within 30 days of the filing, obtain an official seal that includes the name of the notary public and the name of the county to which the notary public has transferred, if applicable.

(d) The recording fee specified in Section 27361 of the Government Code shall be paid by the person appointed as a notary public. The fee may be paid to the county clerk who shall transmit it to the county recorder.

(e) The county recorder shall record the bond and shall thereafter mail, unless specified to the contrary, it to the person named in the instrument and, if no person is named, to the party leaving it for recording.

SUMMARY

No more than 30 days after the date of commission, every notary must file an official bond and oath of office with the county clerk where the notary has their place of business, or the commission will not take effect. With proper identification, the notary may take and sign their oath of office before the county clerk or before another notary public. If done before another notary public, that notary public must deliver the oath to the county recorder and to the county clerk who will process it appropriately and keep a copy of it on file for one year. If a notary moves their primary business location, the notary public may choose to file a new oath of office and bond in the new county or a duplicate of the original oath and bond in the new county. If the notary chooses to make a new filing, the notary public must obtain a new seal showing the new county within 30 days.

If a notary public applies for name change, the notary public must file a new oath of office and an amendment to the bond with the county clerk in the county where the notary's place of business is located within 30 days. If the place of business moves to a new county, the notary public must file an amended bond and a new oath with the clerk in the new county. Within 30 days afterward, the notary public must obtain a new seal which reflects their new name and, if applicable, new county. The notary public shall pay for the appropriate recordation fees incurred and, once recorded, the county recorder shall mail the recorded bond to the notary public.

TRUE OR FALSE?

54.   A notary public's appointment is valid only if an oath of office and $15,000.00 surety bond have been filed with the county clerk within 30 calendar days.

✓ Answer key on Page 222

§ 8213.5. Change in location or address of business or residence; notice

A notary public shall notify the Secretary of State by certified mail or any other means of physical delivery that provides a receipt within 30 days as to any change in the location or address of the principal place of business or residence. A notary public shall not use a commercial mail receiving agency or post office box as his or her principal place of business or residence unless the notary public also provides the Secretary of State with a physical street address as the principal place of residence. Willful failure to notify the Secretary of State of a change of address shall be punishable as an infraction by a fine of not more than five hundred dollars ($500).

SUMMARY

A notary public must notify the Secretary of State of any address change in writing within 30 days and send such notice via certified mail or any delivery method that provides a receipt. A notary public may not use a commercial mail receiving agency as a business address unless he/she has provided the Secretary of State with a physical street address for their residence. Intentional failure to notify the Secretary of State of an address change may be punished by a fine of no more than $500.00.

TRUE OR FALSE?

55.   A notary public may list a commercial mail receiving agency as their place of business as long as it is not a postal box.

✓ Answer key on Page 222

§ 8213.6. Name changes; application; filing

If a notary public changes his or her name, the notary public shall complete an application for name change form and file that application with the Secretary of State. Information on this form shall be subject to the confidentiality provisions described in Section 8201.5. Upon approval of the name change form, the Secretary of State shall issue a commission that reflects the new name of the notary public. The term of the commission and commission number shall remain the same. Willful failure to notify the Secretary of State of a name change shall be punishable as an infraction by a fine of not more than five hundred dollars ($500).

SUMMARY

If a notary public changes their name, the notary must file an application for name change with the Secretary of State. The new name will be held in the same confidence as their former name. Once approved, the Secretary of State shall issue a new commission certificate showing the new name along with the same commission date and number. The notary's deliberate failure to do so may be punishable by a fine of no more than $500.00.

TRUE OR FALSE?

56.   A notary public who changes their name and submits an application to the Secretary of State will have their commission reset to the date that the application was approval on.

✓ Answer key on Page 222

§ 8214. Misconduct or neglect

For the official misconduct or neglect of a notary public, the notary public and the sureties on the notary public's official bond are liable in a civil action to the persons injured thereby for all the damages sustained.

SUMMARY

If a notary public commits official misconduct or neglect, the notary public and their surety bond are financially responsible for compensation ordered in a lawsuit brought by any victim of the misconduct or neglect.

TRUE OR FALSE?

57.   A notary public won't have to pay out of their own pocket for negligence or misconduct as long as he/she has a surety bond to cover it.

✓ Answer key on Page 222

§ 8214.1. Grounds for refusal, revocation or suspension of commission

The Secretary of State may refuse to appoint any person as notary public or may revoke or suspend the commission of any notary public upon any of the following grounds:

(a) Substantial and material misstatement or omission in the application submitted to the Secretary of State to become a notary public.

(b) Conviction of a felony, a lesser offense involving moral turpitude, or a lesser offense of a nature incompatible with the duties of a notary public. A conviction after a plea of nolo contendere is deemed to be a conviction within the meaning of this subdivision.

(c) Revocation, suspension, restriction, or denial of a professional license, if the revocation, suspension, restriction, or denial was for misconduct based on dishonesty, or for any cause substantially relating to the duties or responsibilities of a notary public.

(d) Failure to discharge fully and faithfully any of the duties or responsibilities required of a notary public.

(e) When adjudicated liable for damages in any suit grounded in fraud, misrepresentation, or for a violation of the state regulatory laws, or in any suit based upon a failure to discharge fully and faithfully the duties as a notary public.

(f) The use of false or misleading advertising wherein the notary public has represented that the notary public has duties, rights, or privileges that he or she does not possess by law.

(g) The practice of law in violation of Section 6125 of the Business and Professions Code.

(h) Charging more than the fees prescribed by this chapter.

(i) Commission of any act involving dishonesty, fraud, or deceit with the intent to substantially benefit the notary public or another, or substantially injure another.

(j) Failure to complete the acknowledgment at the time the notary's signature and seal are affixed to the document.

(k) Failure to administer the oath or affirmation as required by paragraph (3) of subdivision of Section 8205.

(l) Execution of any certificate as a notary public containing a statement known to the notary public to be false.

(m) Violation of Section 8223.

(n) Failure to submit any remittance payable upon demand by the Secretary of State under this chapter or failure to satisfy any court-ordered money judgment, including restitution.

(o) Failure to secure the sequential journal of official acts, pursuant to Section 8206, or the official seal, pursuant to Section 8207, or willful failure to report the theft or loss of the sequential journal, pursuant to subdivision (b) of Section 8206.

(p) Violation of Section 8219.5.

(q) Commission of an act in violation of Section 6203, 8214.2, 8225, or 8227.3 of the Government Code or of Section 115, 470, 487, subdivision (a) of Section 487a, or Section 530.5 of the Penal Code.

(r) Willful failure to provide access to the sequential journal of official acts upon request by a peace officer.

SUMMARY

The Secretary of State may refuse to appoint a person as a notary public or revoke/suspend their commission for the following reasons:

(a) Significantly false or omitted information in the application.

(b) Conviction of a felony, or a lesser offense of moral corruption, or a lesser offense for any crime which conflicts with the duties of a notary public. Any conviction following a plea of "no contest" is considered a conviction as it applies to this paragraph.

(c) Denial, restriction, or revocation of a professional license for misconduct involving dishonesty or trustworthiness.

(d) Failure to lawfully perform the duties of the office of notary public.

(e) If the person has been found guilty of fraud, misrepresentation, conviction of any offense involving moral depravity, regulatory violations or failure to perform the duties of a notary public lawfully and honestly.

(f) Misleading advertising by the notary public to claim legal authority or powers they does not actually have.

(g) The unauthorized practice of law.

(h) Charging more than the maximum fees allowed by law.

(i) Committing any dishonest, fraudulent, or deceitful act with the intent to benefit themselves or injure another person.

(j) Failing to complete the acknowledgment on a document at the same time the notary seal and signature are made on the document.

(k) Failure to administer the oath as required on an oath or affirmation.

(l) Performing a notarial act on an instrument with any content the notary public knows to be false.

(m) Violating any code governing the notary public's role and duties in immigration-related matters.

(n) Failure to pay any fees demanded by the Secretary of State or paying any judgment for monetary fees, fines, or restitution ordered by a court.

(o) Failure to keep the notary public journal secure and accessible by the notary public alone, or failure to report the theft of a notary journal.

(p) Failing to display the appropriate bilingual signage by any notary public who notarizes in English and any other language.

(q) Committing any act involving assault or abuse, fraud involving a deed of trust, improper notarial act, forgery or misrepresentation.

(r) Refusal to provide access of their notary journal upon request by a peace officer.

TRUE OR FALSE?

58.   The Secretary of State may revoke the commission of a notary public if the notary had their CPA license revoked for non-criminal reasons.

✓ Answer key on Page 222

§ 8214.15. Civil penalties

(a) In addition to any commissioning or disciplinary sanction, a violation of subdivision (f), (i), (l), (m), or (p) of Section 8214.1, or a willful violation of subdivision (d) of Section 8214.1, is punishable by a civil penalty not to exceed one thousand five hundred dollars ($1,500).

(b) In addition to any commissioning or disciplinary sanction, a violation of subdivision (h), (j), or (k) of Section 8214.1, or a negligent violation of subdivision (d) of Section 8214.1 is punishable by a civil penalty not to exceed seven hundred fifty dollars ($750).

(c) The civil penalty may be imposed by the Secretary of State if a hearing is not requested pursuant to Section 8214.3. If a hearing is requested, the hearing officer shall make the determination.

(d) Any civil penalties collected pursuant to this section shall be transferred to the General Fund. It is the intent of the Legislature that to the extent General Fund moneys are raised by penalties collected pursuant to this section, that money shall be made available to the Secretary of State's office to defray its costs of investigating and pursuing commissioning and monetary remedies for violations of the notary public law.

SUMMARY

(a) If a notary public violates subdivision (f), (i), (l), (m), or (p) of Section 8214.1, or deliberately violates subdivision (d) of Section 8214.1 the notary public is subject to a civil penalty in an amount no more than $1,500.00 in addition to any commissioning or disciplinary action.

(b) If a notary public violates subdivision (h), (j), or (k) of Section 8214.1, or negligently violates subdivision (d) of Section 8214.1 the notary public is subject to a civil penalty in an amount no more than $750.00 in addition to any additional commission or disciplinary action.

(c) Civil penalties may be imposed by the Secretary of State unless a hearing is requested by the notary public, in which case the hearing officer shall make the determination on any civil penalty(ies).

(d) Any civil penalties collected pursuant to this section shall be transferred to the General Fund to mitigate the Secretary of State's expenses incurred in investigating and prosecuting acts of notarial misconduct.

TRUE OR FALSE?

59.   The Secretary of State may impose civil penalties as long as no hearing has been requested.

✓ Answer key on Page 222

§ 8214.2. Fraud relating to deed of trust; single-family residence; felony

(a) A notary public who knowingly and willfully with intent to defraud performs any notarial act in relation to a deed of trust on real property consisting of a single-family residence containing not more than four dwelling units, with knowledge that the deed of trust contains any false statements or is forged, in whole or in part, is guilty of a felony.

(b) The penalty provided by this section is not an exclusive remedy and does not affect any other relief or remedy provided by law.

SUMMARY

(a) A notary public is guilty of a felony if the notary public deliberately commits fraud by performing a notarial act involving a deed of trust for real property with a single-family home on it and knows the deed is false, invalid, or forged.

(b) The penalty for this fraud does not prevent prosecution of the notary public and the award of any other relief or remedy provided by law.

TRUE OR FALSE?

60.   If a notary public knows the legal description of a deed of trust has been altered but the signer has promised to pay the notary to "look the other way", the notary has committed a felony.

✓ Answer key on Page 222

§ 8214.21. Failure to provide access to the sequential journal of notarial acts; civil penalties

A notary public who willfully fails to provide access to the sequential journal of notarial acts when requested by a peace officer shall be subject to a civil penalty not exceeding two thousand five hundred dollars ($2,500). An action to impose a civil penalty under this subdivision may be brought by the Secretary of State in an administrative proceeding or any public prosecutor in superior court and shall be enforced as a civil judgment. A public prosecutor shall inform the secretary of any civil penalty imposed under this section.

SUMMARY

A notary public who refuses to allow access to their notary journal upon request by a peace officer is subject to fine of no more than $2,500.00. Punitive action against the notary public for such refusal may be initiated by the Secretary of State or any public prosecutor to enforce it as a judgment.

TRUE OR FALSE?

61.   If a police officer requests review of a notary public's journal, the notary public may reject the request if it's for a really good reason.

✓ Answer key on Page 222

§ 8214.23. Failure to obtain thumbprint; civil penalties; limitations

Notwithstanding any other limitation of time described in Section 802 of the Penal Code, or any other provision of law, prosecution for a violation of this offense shall be commenced within four years after discovery of the commission of the offense, or within four years after the completion of the offense, whichever is later.

SUMMARY

A notary public who fails to obtain a thumbprint from the signer when necessary is subject to a fine of no more than $2,500.00. Punitive action against the notary public for such refusal may be initiated by the Secretary of State or any public prosecutor to enforce it as a judgment. There is a time limit to bring action against a notary public's violation of this section as follows: four years from the date of discovery of the violation or within four years after completion of the violation, whichever is later.

TRUE OR FALSE?

62. If a notary public does not obtain a signer's thumbprint on a power of attorney, there is no violation because the thumbprint is optional.

✓ Answer key on Page 222

§ 8214.3. Hearing prior to denial or revocation of commission or imposition of civil penalties; law governing; exceptions

Prior to a revocation or suspension pursuant to this chapter or after a denial of a commission, or prior to the imposition of a civil penalty, the person affected shall have a right to a hearing on the matter and the proceeding shall be conducted in accordance with Chapter 5 (commencing with Section 11500) of Part 1 of Division 3, except that a person shall not have a right to a hearing after a denial of an application for a notary public commission in either of the following cases:

(a) The Secretary of State has, within one year previous to the application, and after proceedings conducted in accordance with Chapter 5 (commencing with Section 11500) of Part 1 of Division 3, denied or revoked the applicant's application or commission.

(b) The Secretary of State has entered an order pursuant to Section 8214.4 finding that the applicant has committed or omitted acts constituting grounds for suspension or revocation of a notary public's commission.

SUMMARY

Prior to any disciplinary action or penalty imposed against a notary public or applicant, the individual is entitled to a hearing which shall be governed by Chapter 5 (commencing with Section 11500) of Part 1 of Division 3, with the following exceptions:

(a) The Secretary of State has denied or revoked an applicant's application or commission within one year prior to the application.

(b) The Secretary of State has entered an order finding the applicant has committed or omitted acts which are grounds for suspension or revocation of a notary public's commission.

TRUE OR FALSE?

63. A notary public or applicant is always entitled to have a fair hearing on any adverse action taken by the Secretary of State against the notary or applicant.

✓ Answer key on Page 222

§ 8214.4. Resignation or expiration of commission not a bar to investigation or disciplinary proceedings

Notwithstanding this chapter or Chapter 5 (commencing with Section 11500) of Part 1 of Division 3, if the Secretary of State determines, after proceedings conducted in accordance with Chapter 5 (commencing with Section 11500) of Part 1 of Division 3, that any notary public has committed or omitted acts constituting grounds for suspension or revocation of a notary public's commission, the resignation or expiration of the notary public's commission shall not bar the Secretary of State from instituting or continuing an investigation or instituting disciplinary proceedings. Upon completion of the disciplinary proceedings, the Secretary of State shall enter an order finding the facts and stating the conclusion that the facts would or would not have constituted grounds for suspension or revocation of the commission if the commission had still been in effect.

SUMMARY

A notary public's resignation of their commission or the expiration of their commission does not prevent the Secretary of State from initiating/continuing an investigation against the notary public or initiating/continuing disciplinary proceedings against the notary public. Once the disciplinary proceedings are completed, the Secretary of State shall enter an order with the facts of the matter explained and a statement that those facts would have resulted in the suspension or revocation of the notary public's commission if it was still in effect.

TRUE OR FALSE?

64. A notary public cannot avoid disciplinary action and penalties by resigning their commission or letting it expire.

✓ Answer key on Page 222

§ 8214.5. Revocation of commission; filing copy with county clerk

Whenever the Secretary of State revokes the commission of any notary public, the Secretary of State shall file with the county clerk of the county in which the notary public's principal place of business is located a copy of the revocation. The county clerk shall note such revocation and its date upon the original record of such certificate.

SUMMARY

When a Secretary of State revokes a notary public's commission, the Secretary of State shall also file a copy of the revocation with the county clerk where the notary's principal place of business is located. The county clerk shall note the revocation and date upon the original certificate.

TRUE OR FALSE?

65.   If the Secretary of State revokes a notary public's commission, a copy of the revocation must be filed with the clerk of the county where the notary public does business.

✓ Answer key on Page 222

§ 8214.8.   Revocation upon certain convictions

Upon conviction of any offense in this chapter, or of Section 6203, or of any felony, of a person commissioned as a notary public, in addition to any other penalty, the court shall revoke the commission of the notary public and shall require the notary public to surrender to the court the seal of the notary public. The court shall forward the seal, together with a certified copy of the judgment of conviction, to the Secretary of State.

SUMMARY

A notary public convicted of any offense in this chapter, or Section 6203, or a felony shall have their commission revoked by the court in addition to any other penalty. The court shall require the notary public to surrender their seal. The court shall then forward the seal and a certified copy of the judgment or conviction to the Secretary of State.

TRUE OR FALSE?

66.   If a court of law revokes the commission of a notary public, the notary must surrender their official seal to the court.

✓ Answer key on Page 222

§ 8216. Release of surety

When a surety of a notary desires to be released from responsibility on account of future acts, the release shall be pursuant to Article 11 (commencing with Section 996.110), and not by cancellation or withdrawal pursuant to Article 13 (commencing with Section 996.310), of Chapter 2 of Title 14 of Part 2 of the Code of Civil Procedure. For this purpose, the surety shall make application to the superior court of the county in which the notary public's principal place of business is located and the copy of the application and notice of hearing shall be served on the Secretary of State as the beneficiary.

SUMMARY

When a surety of a notary wishes to be released from any responsibility for a notary's future acts, the surety shall apply to the superior court of the county in which the notary's place of business is located. The surety must then serve a copy of the application and notice of hearing on the Secretary of State as the beneficiary.

TRUE OR FALSE?

67.   A surety must initiate its application with the Secretary of State to be released from any future responsibility for a notary public's acts.

✓ Answer key on Page 222

§ 8219.5. Advertising in language other than English; posting of notice relating to legal advice and fees; translation of notary public into Spanish; suspension

(a) Every notary public who is not an attorney who advertises the services of a notary public in a language other than English by signs or other means of written communication, with the exception of a single desk plaque, shall post with that advertisement a notice in English and in the other language which sets forth the following:
(1) This statement: I am not an attorney and, therefore, cannot give legal advice about immigration or any other legal matters.
(2) The fees set by statute which a notary public may charge.
(b) The notice required by subdivision (a) shall be printed and posted as prescribed by the Secretary of State.
(c) Literal translation of the phrase "notary public" into Spanish, hereby defined as "notario

publico" or "notario," is prohibited. For purposes of this subdivision, "literal translation" of a word or phrase from one language to another means the translation of a word or phrase without regard to the true meaning of the word or phrase in the language which is being translated.

(d) The Secretary of State shall suspend for a period of not less than one year or revoke the commission of any notary public who fails to comply with subdivision (a) or (c). However, on the second offense the commission of such notary public shall be revoked permanently.

SUMMARY

If a non-attorney notary public advertises notarial services in a language other than English, then the notary public is required by law to post a bilingual notice in English and the other language stating that the notary public is not an attorney and cannot give legal advice of any kind. A list of the statutory fees a California notary public may charge must also be posted. A notary public is prohibited from translating the term "Notary Public," into Spanish (defined as "notario publico" or "notario") even with the mandatory bilingual notice posted.

A first offense violation of this law may result in immediate suspension or revocation of the notary public's commission. A second offense violation of this law may result in immediate and permanent revocation of the notary public's commission.

TRUE OR FALSE?

68.   A notary public may notarize immigration documents for a signer but may not answer any questions the signer asks about the paperwork.

✓ Answer key on Page 222

§ 8220. Rules and regulations

The Secretary of State may adopt rules and regulations to carry out the provisions of this chapter.
The regulations shall be adopted in accordance with the Administrative Procedure Act (Chapter 3.5 (commencing with Section 11340) of Part 1 of Division 3).

SUMMARY

The Secretary of State may update, add, or remove rules and regulations to carry out the provisions of this chapter. The regulations shall be adopted in accordance with the Administrative Procedure Act (Chapter 3.5 (commencing with Section 11340) of Part 1 of Division 3).

TRUE OR FALSE?

69.   The Secretary of State may create and/or implement rules and regulations if they are deemed necessary to govern matters related to notaries public.

✓   Answer key on Page 222

§ 8221. Destruction, defacement or concealment of records or papers; misdemeanor; liability for damages

If any person shall knowingly destroy, deface, or conceal any records or papers belonging to the office of a notary public, such person shall be guilty of a misdemeanor and be liable in a civil action for damages to any person injured as a result of such destruction, defacing, or concealment.

Notwithstanding any other limitation of time described in Section 802 of the Penal Code, or any other provision of law, prosecution for a violation of this offense shall be commenced within four years after discovery of the commission of the offense, or within four years after the completion of the offense, whichever is later. The penalty provided by this section is not an exclusive remedy and does not affect any other relief or remedy provided by law.

SUMMARY

If anyone deliberately destroys, defaces, or conceals any records belonging to a notary public, that person is guilty of a misdemeanor and subject to a civil lawsuit for monetary damages payable to anyone adversely affected by the destruction, defacing, or concealment. Prosecution of a person for this violation must begin within four years after the offense is discovered or completed, whichever is later. This provision does not affect or prohibit any other time limit or legal remedy available.

TRUE OR FALSE?

70.   If a person is found to have purposely shredded a notary journal six years ago, he/she cannot be prosecuted or fined their actions because it has been more than four years.

✓ Answer key on Page 222

§ 8222. Injunction; reimbursement for expenses

(a) Whenever it appears to the Secretary of State that any person has engaged or is about to engage in any acts or practices which constitute or will constitute a violation of any provision of this chapter or any rule or regulation prescribed under the authority thereof, the Secretary of State may apply for an injunction, and upon a proper showing, any court of competent jurisdiction has power to issue a permanent or temporary injunction or restraining order to enforce the provisions of this chapter, and any party to the action has the right to prosecute an appeal from the order or judgment of the court.

(b) The court may order a person subject to an injunction or restraining order provided for in this section to reimburse the Secretary of State for expenses incurred in the investigation related to the petition. The Secretary of State shall refund any amount received as reimbursement should the injunction or restraining order be dissolved by an appellate court.

SUMMARY

If the Secretary of State believes a person is, has, or will commit a violation of any rule, regulation or code governing notaries and notary applicants, the Secretary of State may obtain a temporary or permanent injunction or restraining order against that person. The person bound by the injunction or restraining order may pursue an appeal for relief from the court order or injunction. The court may order the person subject to an injunction or restraining order to reimburse the Secretary of State for the costs of investigation, however, the Secretary of State must refund the payment back to the person if the injunction or restraining order is found improper and dissolved by an appellate court.

TRUE OR FALSE?

71.   A person who has been restricted by an injunction or restraining order may appeal the injunction or restraining order to have it dissolved.

✓ Answer key on Page 222

§ 8223. Notary public with expertise in immigration matters; advertising status as notary public; entry of information on forms; fee limitations

(a) A notary public who holds himself or herself out as being an immigration specialist, immigration consultant, or any other title or description reflecting an expertise in immigration matters shall not advertise in any manner whatsoever that he or she is a notary public.

(b) A notary public qualified and bonded as an immigration consultant under Chapter 19.5 (commencing with Section 22440) of Division 8 of the Business and Professions Code may enter data, provided by the client, on immigration forms provided by a federal or state agency. The fee for this service shall not exceed fifteen dollars ($15) per individual for each set of forms. If notary services are performed in relation to the set of immigration forms, additional fees may be collected pursuant to Section 8211. This fee limitation shall not apply to an attorney, who is also a notary public, who is rendering professional services regarding immigration matters.

(c) This section shall not be construed to exempt a notary public who enters data on an immigration form at the direction of a client, or otherwise performs the services of an immigration consultant, as defined by Section 22441 of the Business and Professions Code, from the requirements of Chapter 19.5 (commencing with Section 22440) of Division 8 of the Business and Professions Code. A notary public who is not qualified and bonded as an immigration consultant under Chapter 19.5 (commencing with Section 22440) of Division 8 of the Business and Professions Code may not enter data provided by a client on immigration forms nor otherwise perform the services of an immigration consultant.

SUMMARY

If a notary public advertises as an immigration specialist or consultant, he/she is prohibited from disclosing their status as a notary public. If the notary public is registered by the California Secretary of State and bonded as an immigration consultant under the Business and Professions Code, the notary may enter data, provided by the client, on immigration forms, provided by a federal or state agency. The notary may not charge more than $15.00 per individual for each set of forms. If notary services are also performed on the set of immigration forms, the notary may charge additional fees no more than fifteen dollars ($15.00) per set, unless the notary is also an attorney who is rendering professional services as an attorney.

This section does not create an exemption for any notary public who is not qualified and bonded as an immigration consultant. The notary may not enter data provided by a client on immigration forms nor perform the services of an immigration consultant.

TRUE OR FALSE?

72. A notary public must voluntarily terminate their notary public commission if he/she

becomes an immigration specialist or consultant.

✓ Answer key on Page 222

§ 8224. Conflict of interest; financial or beneficial interest in transaction; exceptions

A notary public who has a direct financial or beneficial interest in a transaction shall not perform any notarial act in connection with such transaction. For purposes of this section, a notary public has a direct financial or beneficial interest in a transaction if the notary public:

(a) With respect to a financial transaction, is named, individually, as a principal to the transaction.

(b) With respect to real property, is named, individually, as a grantor, grantee, mortgagor, mortgagee, trustor, trustee, beneficiary, vendor, vendee, lessor, or lessee, to the transaction.

For purposes of this section, a notary public has no direct financial or beneficial interest in a transaction where the notary public acts in the capacity of an agent, employee, insurer, attorney, escrow, or lender for a person having a direct financial or beneficial interest in the transaction.

SUMMARY

A notary public is prohibited from notarizing documents that the notary is named as a principal party to a financial transaction; and/or the notary is named as a beneficiary, grantor, grantee, mortgagor, mortgagee, trustor, trustee, vendor, vendee, lessor, or lessee to a real property transaction. If the notary is acting in the capacity of an agent, employee, insurer, attorney, escrow holder, or lender and has no direct financial or beneficial interest then the notary may perform notarial acts to the transactions.

TRUE OR FALSE?

73. A notary public may notarize the signature of relatives or anyone else as long as the document being signed doesn't benefit the notary public in any way.

✓ Answer key on Page 222

§ 8224.1. Writings, depositions or affidavits of notary public; prohibitions against proof or taking by that notary public

A notary public shall not take the acknowledgment or proof of instruments of writing executed by the notary public nor shall depositions or affidavits of the notary public be taken by the notary public.

SUMMARY

A notary public is prohibited from notarizing their own signature and is also prohibited from taking depositions or affidavits of their own testimony.

§ 8225. Improper notarial acts, solicitation, coercion or influence of performance; misdemeanor

(a) Any person who solicits, coerces, or in any manner influences a notary public to perform an improper notarial act knowing that act to be an improper notarial act, including any act required of a notary public under Section 8206, shall be guilty of a misdemeanor.

(b) Notwithstanding any other limitation of time described in Section 802 of the Penal Code, or any other provision of law, prosecution for a violation of this offense shall be commenced within four years after discovery of the commission of the offense, or within four years after the completion of the offense, whichever is later.

(c) The penalty provided by this section is not an exclusive remedy and does not affect any other relief or remedy provided by law.

SUMMARY

Any person who knowingly influences or attempts to influence a notary public to perform an improper notarial act is guilty of a misdemeanor. Prosecution of a person for this violation must begin within four years after the offense is discovered or completed, whichever is later. This provision does not affect or prohibit any other time limit or legal remedy available for prosecution.

TRUE OR FALSE?

74. A person who has intimidated a notary public into performing a prohibited notarial act is guilty of a misdemeanor under this code but may be charged and prosecuted for a more severe offense with greater penalties.

✓ Answer key on Page 222

§ 8227.1. Unlawful acts by one not a notary public; misdemeanor

It shall be a misdemeanor for any person who is not a duly commissioned, qualified, and acting notary public for the State of California to do any of the following:
- (a) Represent or hold himself or herself out to the public or to any person as being entitled to act as a notary public.
- (b) Assume, use or advertise the title of notary public in such a manner as to convey the impression that the person is a notary public.
- (c) Purport to act as a notary public.

SUMMARY

Anyone who is not a lawfully commissioned notary public for the state of California is guilty of a misdemeanor if the person states they are a notary public; advertises or implies they are a notary public; and/or poses as a notary public.

TRUE OR FALSE?

75.   A person who has applied to the Secretary of State for a notary public commission may advertise as a notary public while awaiting approval.

✓ Answer key on Page 222

§ 8227.3. Unlawful acts by one not a notary public; deeds of trust on single-family residences; felony

Any person who is not a duly commissioned, qualified, and acting notary public who does any of the acts prohibited by Section 8227.1 in relation to any document or instrument affecting title to, placing an encumbrance on, or placing an interest secured by a mortgage or deed of trust on, real property consisting of a single-family residence containing not more than four dwelling units, is guilty of a felony.

SUMMARY

Anyone who is not a notary public but posing as a notary public in any transaction involving a document or instrument which creates a debt, lien, or mortgage obligation on real property consisting of a single-family residence is guilty of a felony.

TRUE OR FALSE?

76.   If Sean says he is a notary public, but isn't a notary public and he notarizes a mortgage loan contract on a home, he is guilty of a felony.

✓ Answer key on Page 222

§ 8228. Enforcement of chapter; examination of notarial books, records, etc.

The Secretary of State or a peace officer, as defined in Sections 830.1, 830.2, and 830.3 of the Penal Code, possessing reasonable suspicion and acting in his or her official capacity and within his or her authority, may enforce the provisions of this chapter through the examination of a notary public's books, records, letters, contracts, and other pertinent documents relating to the official acts of the notary public.

SUMMARY

The Secretary of State or a peace officer acting in their official capacity and authority with reasonable suspicion, may enforce the codes, rules, and regulations governing notaries public by examining a notary public's books, records, letters, contracts, and other pertinent documents related to the official acts of the notary public.

TRUE OR FALSE?

77.   A notary public's journals and all documentation are subject to review and inspection by any peace officer or the Secretary of State upon demand.

✓ Answer key on Page 222

§ 8228.1. Willful failure to perform duty or control notarial seal

(a) Any notary public who willfully fails to perform any duty required of a notary public under Section 8206, or who willfully fails to keep the seal of the notary public under the direct and exclusive control of the notary public, or who surrenders the seal of the notary public to any person not otherwise authorized by law to possess the seal of the notary, shall be guilty of a misdemeanor.

(b) Notwithstanding any other limitation of time described in Section 802 of the Penal Code or any other provision of law, prosecution for a violation of this offense shall be commenced within four years after discovery of the commission of the offense, or within four years after the completion of the offense, whichever is later.

(c) The penalty provided by this section is not an exclusive remedy and does not affect any other relief or remedy provided by law.

SUMMARY

It is a misdemeanor offense for a notary public to deliberately fail to perform a notarial duty under Section 8206; deliberately fail to keep their notary seal under their own sole and secured control; and/or deliberately surrender their notary seal to any person not otherwise authorized by law to possess the seal. Prosecution of a notary for this violation must begin within four years after the offense is discovered or completed, whichever is later. This provision does not affect or prohibit any other time limit or legal remedy available for prosecution.

TRUE OR FALSE?

78.   A notary public's failure to keep their seal secured where only he/she can access it is a misdemeanor.

✓ Answer key on Page 222

§ 8230. Identification of affiant; verification

If a notary public executes a jurat and the statement sworn or subscribed to is contained in a document purporting to identify the affiant, and includes the birthdate or age of the person and a purported photograph or finger or thumbprint of the person so swearing or subscribing, the notary public shall require, as a condition to executing the jurat, that the person verify the birthdate or age contained in the statement by showing either:

(a) A certified copy of the person's birth certificate, or

(b) An identification card or driver's license issued by the Department of Motor Vehicles. For the purposes of preparing for submission of forms required by the United States Immigration and Naturalization Service, and only for such purposes, a notary public may also accept for identification any documents or declarations acceptable to the United States Immigration and Naturalization Service.

SUMMARY

If a notary public signs a jurat on a document stating the identity of the signer and the document cites the birth date or age of the signer with a photograph or finger/thumb print of the signer, the notary shall require proof of the signer's birthdate and age with a certified copy of the signer's birth certificate or an ID card/driver's license issued by the Department of Motor Vehicles. If the notarial act is being performed for the purpose of submitting forms required by the US Immigration and Naturalization Service, a notary public may also accept any documents or declarations acceptable to the US Immigration and Naturalization Service, but ONLY for that purpose and occasion.

TRUE OR FALSE?

79.   Before a notary signs a jurat on a school registration document which states the signer's birth date and age, the notary may accept proof of the signer's birth date and age with a passport ID card or booklet since it is acceptable to the US Immigration and Naturalization Service.

✓ Answer key on Page 222

§ 1360. Necessity of taking constitutional oath

Unless otherwise provided, following any election or appointment and before any officer enters on the duties of his or her office, he or she shall take and subscribe the oath or affirmation set forth in Section 3 of Article XX of the Constitution of California.

SUMMARY

Following any election or appointment and before commencing official duties, any officer— including notaries public—must take and subscribe the oath or affirmation set forth in Section 3 of Article XX of the Constitution of California.

§ 1362. Administration by authorized officer

Unless otherwise provided, the oath may be taken before any officer authorized to administer oaths.

SUMMARY

This section is self-explanatory and won't be covered with a summary or a true false question.

§ 6100. Performance of services; officers; notaries public

Officers of the state, or of a county or judicial district, shall not perform any official services unless upon the payment of the fees prescribed by law for the performance of the services, except as provided in this chapter.

This section shall not be construed to prohibit any notary public, except a notary public whose fees are required by law to be remitted to the state or any other public agency, from performing notarial services without charging a fee.

SUMMARY

Notaries can only provide notarial services when they receive payment for those services. This section does not prevent any notary public from performing notarial services without a fee, except a notary public whose fees are required by law to be collected and remitted to their employer or agency.

TRUE OR FALSE?

80.   A notary public has full authority to decide whether or not to accept payment for notarial acts.

✓ Answer key on Page 222

§ 6106. Pensions

Neither the State, nor any county or city, nor any public officer or body acting in his official capacity on behalf of the State, any county, or city, including notaries public, shall receive any fee or compensation for services rendered in an affidavit, or application relating to the securing of a pension, or the payment of a pension voucher, or any matter relating thereto.

SUMMARY

No one, including a notary public, may charge or collect a fee or compensation for services rendered in relation to the securing of a pension or the payment of a pension voucher.

TRUE OR FALSE?

81.   Any official act provided by a notary public for someone securing their pension must be performed at no charge unless the notary public is required to remit fees to their employer.

✓ Answer key on Page 222

§ 6107. Veterans

(a) A public entity, including the state, a county, city, or other political subdivision, or any officer or employee thereof, including notaries public, shall not demand or receive any fee or compensation for doing any of the following:

   (1) Recording, indexing, or issuing certified copies of any discharge, certificate of service, certificate of satisfactory service, notice of separation, or report of separation of any member of the Armed Forces of the United States.

   (2) Furnishing a certified copy of, or searching for, any public record that is to be used in an application or claim for a pension, allotment, allowance, compensation, insurance (including automatic insurance), or any other benefits under any act of Congress for service in the Armed Forces of the United States or under any law of this state relating to veterans' benefits.

   (3) Furnishing a certified copy of, or searching for, any public record that is required by the Veterans Administration to be used in determining the eligibility of any person to participate in benefits made available by the Veterans Administration.

   (4) Rendering any other service in connection with an application or claim referred to in paragraph (2) or (3).

(b) A certified copy of any record referred to in subdivision (a) may be made available only to one of the following:

   (1) The person who is the subject of the record upon presentation of proper photo identification.

   (2) A family member or legal representative of the person who is the subject of the record upon presentation of proper photo identification and certification of their relationship to the subject of the record.

   (3) A state, county, or city office that provides veteran's benefits services upon written request of that office.

   (4) A United States official upon written request of that official. A public officer or employee is liable on his or her official bond for failure or refusal to render the services.

SUMMARY

No one, including a notary public, may charge or collect a fee or compensation for services rendered in relation to acquiring, certifying, copying, or any other processing of documents required by the Veterans Administration for securing any veterans benefits. The documents or services may be made available to only the following persons: the person who is the subject of the record; a family member or legal representative for the person who is the subject of the record; a state, county, or city office that provides veterans benefits; and a US official upon written request.

TRUE OR FALSE?

82.   A notary public is prohibited from charging or collecting a fee to notarize a veteran's signature on their certificate of title to sell their vehicle.

✓ Answer key on Page 222

§ 6108. Oaths of office; claim against counties

No officer of a county or judicial district shall charge or receive any fee or compensation for administering or certifying the oath of office or for filing or swearing to any claim or demand against any county in the State.

SUMMARY

No officer of a county or judicial district—including notaries public—may charge or receive compensation for administering or certifying the oath of office or for filing/swearing to any claim or demand against any county in the state.

TRUE OR FALSE?

83.   A notary public must administer an oath of office to another public official at no charge.

✓ Answer key on Page 222

§ 6109. Receipt of fees; written account; officer liability

Every officer of a county or judicial district, upon receiving any fees for official duty or service, may be required by the person paying the fees to make out in writing and to deliver to the person a particular account of the fees. The account shall specify for what the fees, respectively, accrued, and the officer shall receipt it. If the officer refuses or neglects to do so when required, he is liable to the person paying the fees in treble the amount so paid.

SUMMARY

Every county or judicial district officer—including notaries public—may be required to provide a receipt to a person who has paid a fee to the officer, showing a full accounting of what was paid and for what services.

TRUE OR FALSE?

84.   If required, a notary public must provide a detailed receipt for the official acts performed by the notary for the signer.

✓ Answer key on Page 222

§ 6110. Performance of services following payment; officer liability

Upon payment of the fees required by law, the officer shall perform the services required. For every failure or refusal to do so, the officer is liable upon his official bond.

SUMMARY

When a public officer—including notaries public—receives payment of fees required by law, he/she must perform the services required. If he/she fails or refuses to do so, the officer will be subject to a claim against his official bond.

TRUE OR FALSE?

85.   Once a notary public is paid a fee to notarize a document, he/she is obligated to perform the notarization even if the document is obviously incomplete.

✓ Answer key on Page 222

§ 6203. False certificate or writing by officer

(a) Every officer authorized by law to make or give any certificate or other writing is guilty of a misdemeanor if he or she makes and delivers as true any certificate or writing containing statements which he or she knows to be false.

(b) Notwithstanding any other limitation of time described in Section 802 of the Penal Code, or any other provision of law, prosecution for a violation of this offense shall be commenced within four years after discovery of the commission of the offense, or within four years after the completion of the offense, whichever is later.

(c) The penalty provided by this section is not an exclusive remedy and does not affect any other relief or remedy provided by law.

SUMMARY

Every public officer—including notaries public—authorized to make or issue any certificate or other similar instrument commits a misdemeanor if he/she issues it with statements or information he/she knows to be false. Prosecution of a person for this violation must begin within four years after the offense is discovered or completed, whichever is later. This provision does not affect or prohibit any other time limit or legal remedy available for prosecution.

TRUE OR FALSE?

86.   A notary public is prohibited from notarizing any document which he/she knows to be incomplete or false.

✓ Answer key on Page 222

§ 6800. Computation of time in which act is to be done

The time in which any act provided by law is to be done is computed by excluding the first day, and including the last, unless the last day is a holiday, and then it is also excluded.

SUMMARY

The deadline for any act required by law to be performed in a certain timeframe is determined by excluding the first day, and including the last, unless the last day is a holiday, and then it is also excluded.

EXAMPLE

A notary public sends notice to the Secretary of State that the notary's official seal has been damaged and is unusable. The Secretary of State must issue a certificate of authorization to the notary within five days so the notary may use it to purchase a new seal.

The Secretary of State received the notary public's notice on Thursday, May 9th. To compute the five-day deadline, the public officer in the Secretary of State's office will begin the time computation by excluding the first day (Thursday the 9th) and starting with Friday the 10th as the first day. Saturday the 11th is the second day, Sunday the 12th is the third day, Monday the 13th is the fourth day, and the due date for the officer to issue the certificate of authorization is on the fifth day, Tuesday the 14th. If Tuesday the 14th had been a holiday, then the time computation would have extended to Wednesday the 15th.

§ 27287. Acknowledgment of execution or proof by subscribing witness required before recording; exceptions

* * * before an instrument can be recorded its execution shall be acknowledged by the person executing it, or if executed by a corporation, by its president or secretary or other person executing it on behalf of the corporation, or, except for any power of attorney, quitclaim deed, grant deed, mortgage, deed of trust, security agreement, or other document affecting real property, proved by subscribing witness or as provided in Sections 1198 and 1199 of the Civil Code, and the acknowledgment or proof certified as prescribed by law. This section shall not apply to a trustee's deed resulting from a decree of foreclosure, or a nonjudicial foreclosure pursuant to Section 2924 of the Civil Code, or to a deed of reconveyance.

SUMMARY

Before recording an instrument, the signer must acknowledge signing it, whether the signer is acting as an individual or on behalf of a corporation or other entity; or the signature proved by a subscribing witness on any instrument except any power of attorney, quitclaim deed, grant deed, mortgage, deed of trust, security agreement, or other document affecting real property. This section does not apply to a trustee's deed resulting from a decree of foreclosure, a nonjudicial foreclosure, or a deed a reconveyance.

TRUE OR FALSE?

87.   A person signing a deed of trust may have his signature proven to be authentic by a subscribing witness.

✓ Answer key on Page 222

§ 66433. Content and form; application of article

The content and form of final maps shall be governed by the provisions of this article.

SUMMARY

The content and form of finalized maps must comply with the requirements contained in this article.

§ 66436. Statement of consent; necessity; exceptions; nonliability for omission of signature; notary acknowledgment

(a) A statement, signed and acknowledged by all parties having any record title interest in the subdivided real property, consenting to the preparation and recordation of the final map is required, * * *

(c) A notary acknowledgment shall be deemed complete for recording without the official seal of the notary, so long as the name of the notary, the county of the notary's principal place of business, and the notary's commission expiration date are typed or printed below or immediately adjacent to the notary's signature in the acknowledgment.

SUMMARY

All parties having any record title interest in a subdivided real property must sign and acknowledge a statement consenting to the preparation and recordation of the final map. A notary acknowledgment shall be considered complete for recording without the official seal of the notary, as long as the name of the notary, the county of the notary's principal place of business, and the notary's commission expiration date are typed or printed below or immediately adjacent to the notary's signature.

TRUE OR FALSE?

88.   The signed notary acknowledgment on a finalized map does not require the notary's official seal to be considered complete for recording.

✓ Answer key on Page 222

CIVIL CODE

§ 14. Words and phrases; construction; tense; gender; number

* * * signature or subscription includes mark, when the person cannot write, his name being written near it, by a person who writes his own name as a witness; provided, that when a signature is by mark it must in order that the same may be acknowledged or may serve as the signature to any sworn statement be witnessed by two persons who must subscribe their own names as witnesses thereto. * * *

SUMMARY

If a person is unable to write or sign their name on a document, he/she may sign the document by mark as long as the signer's mark is made in the presence of two additional people who will subscribe their signatures on the document as witnesses. One of the witnesses must print the signer's name next to their mark on the document, then sign their own name in the capacity as a witness. The witnesses are only verifying they observed the person make their mark on the document.

TRUE OR FALSE?

89.   Two persons must witness someone making a mark on the document, but they aren't attesting to the person's identity.

✓ Answer key on Page 222

§ 1181. Notaries public; officers before whom proof or acknowledgment may be made

The proof or acknowledgment of an instrument may be made before a notary public at any place within this state, or within the county or city and county in this state in which the officer specified below was elected or appointed, before either:
(a) A clerk of a superior court.
(b) A county clerk.
(c) A court commissioner.
(d) A retired judge of a municipal or justice court.
(e) A district attorney.
(f) A clerk of a board of supervisors.

(g) A city clerk.

(h) A county counsel.

(i) A city attorney.

(j) Secretary of the Senate.

(k) Chief Clerk of the Assembly.

SUMMARY

The verification of an instrument may be made by its signer to a notary public anywhere in the state or the county or city/county where the following class of officer was elected or appointed:

Reference the class of officer list found in the official section above.

TRUE OR FALSE?

90.   A document verification may be made by the signer to a notary public anywhere in the state.

✓ Answer key on Page 222

§ 1185. Acknowledgments; requisites

(a) The acknowledgment of an instrument shall not be taken unless the officer taking it has satisfactory evidence that the person making the acknowledgment is the individual who is described in and who executed the instrument.

(b) For purposes of this section "satisfactory evidence" means the absence of information, evidence, or other circumstances that would lead a reasonable person to believe that the person making the acknowledgment is not the individual he or she claims to be and any one of the following:

(1) (A) The oath or affirmation of a credible witness personally known to the officer, whose identity is proven to the officer upon presentation of a document satisfying the requirements of paragraph (3) or (4), that the person making the acknowledgment is personally known to the witness and that each of the following are true:

(i)   The person making the acknowledgment is the person named in the document.

(ii)   The person making the acknowledgment is personally known to the witness.

(iii)   That it is the reasonable belief of the witness that the circumstances of the person making the acknowledgment are such that it would be very difficult or impossible for that person to obtain another form of identification.

(iv)   The person making the acknowledgment does not possess any of the identification documents named in paragraphs (3) and (4).

(v) The witness does not have a financial interest in the document being acknowledged and is not named in the document.

(B) A notary public who violates this section by failing to obtain the satisfactory evidence required by subparagraph (A) shall be subject to a civil penalty not exceeding ten thousand dollars ($10,000). An action to impose this civil penalty may be brought by the Secretary of State in an administrative proceeding or a public prosecutor in superior court, and shall be enforced as a civil judgment. A public prosecutor shall inform the secretary of any civil penalty imposed under this subparagraph.

(2) The oath or affirmation under penalty of perjury of two credible witnesses, whose identities are proven to the officer upon the presentation of a document satisfying the requirements to paragraph (3) or (4), that each statement in paragraph (1) is true.

(3) Reasonable reliance on the presentation to the officer of any one of the following, if the document or other form of identification is current or has been issued within five years:

(A) An identification card or driver's license issued by the Department of Motor Vehicles.

(B) A passport issued by the Department of State of the United States.

(C) An inmate identification card issued by the Department of Corrections and Rehabilitation, if the inmate is in custody in prison.

(D) Any form of inmate identification issued by a sheriff's department, if the inmate is in custody in a local detention facility.

(4) Reasonable reliance on the presentation of any one of the following, provided that a document specified in subparagraphs (A) to (F), inclusive, shall either be current or have been issued within five years and shall contain a photograph and description of the person named on it, shall be signed by the person, and shall bear a serial or other identifying number:

(A) A valid consular identification document issued by a consulate from the applicant's country of citizenship, or a valid passport from the applicant's country of citizenship.

(B) A driver's license issued by a state other than California or by a Canadian or Mexican public agency authorized to issue driver's licenses.

(C) An identification card issued by a state other than California.

(D) An identification card issued by any branch of the Armed Forces of the United States.

(E) An employee identification card issued by an agency or office of the State of California, or by an agency or office of a city, county, or city and county in this state.

(F) An identification card issued by a federally recognized tribal government.

(c) An officer who has taken an acknowledgment pursuant to this section shall be presumed to have operated in accordance with the provisions of law.

(d) A party who files an action for damages based on the failure of the officer to establish the proper identity of the person making the acknowledgment shall have the burden of proof in establishing the negligence or misconduct of the officer.

(e) A person convicted of perjury under this section shall forfeit any financial interest in the document.

SUMMARY

The acknowledgment of an instrument shall not be accepted unless the notary public or other officer taking it has satisfactory evidence that the signer is the individual who is described in the document and is the person who signed it. "Satisfactory evidence" means the notary public must determine there is no reason to suspect the person is misrepresenting their identity, AND any of the following:

1. Valid ID documents are described in Civil Code section 1185(b)(3) and (4)).

2. If the person signing the document does not have a valid ID document to present, their identity may be certified by the oath of a single credible witness who personally knows the signer and personally knows the notary public.

    a. The single credible witness must provide the notary public with a valid ID document establishing their own identification.

    b. The single credible witness must swear under oath that the person signing the document is the person named in the document AND the person signing the document is personally known to them, AND the person signing the document has no valid ID and cannot reasonably obtain a valid ID, AND the single credible witness is neither named in the document nor has any financial interest in the document.

3. If the person signing the document does not have a valid ID to present and there is no one qualified to act as a single credible witness, their identity may be certified by the oaths of two credible witnesses who personally know the signer.

    a. The two credible witnesses must provide the notary public with valid ID documents establishing their own identities.

    b. The two credible witnesses must swear under oath that the person signing the document is the same person named in the document AND is personally known to both credible witnesses, AND the person signing the document has no valid ID and cannot reasonably obtain a valid ID, AND affirming the two credible witnesses are neither named in the document nor have any financial interest in the document.

4. Any valid ID document presented to the notary public must be current within the past five years; show a photo of the signer; have a physical description of the signer; show a signature of the signer; and have an identification number assigned by the issuing agency.

5. When presented with a valid ID document during a notarial act, the notary public must record the following in their notary journal: the type of valid ID presented; the issuing agency; the identification number assigned by the issuing agency; and the date of issue or expiration.

6. A notary public and/or any witness may not certify a signer's identity if the notary public and/or witness(es) are named in the document or have a financial interest in the document.

A notary public who violates this section by failing to obtain the satisfactory evidence required to prove identity shall be subject to a civil penalty no greater than $10,000.00. An action to impose this civil penalty may be brought by the Secretary of State in an administrative proceeding or a public prosecutor in superior court and shall be enforced as a civil judgment. A public prosecutor shall inform the secretary of any civil penalty imposed under this subparagraph.

TRUE OR FALSE?

91. A witness does not need to present identification to the notary public when swearing under oath to another signer's identity as long as the witness personally knows the notary public very well.

✓ Answer key on Page 222

§ 1188. Certificate of acknowledgment

An officer taking the acknowledgment of an instrument shall endorse thereon or attach thereto a certificate pursuant to Section 1189.

SUMMARY

An officer taking the acknowledgment of an instrument shall endorse the instrument with a certificate of acknowledgment or attach one to the instrument, according to the form and content described in Section 1189.

TRUE OR FALSE?

92. A notary public who takes an acknowledgement must endorse the instrument with a certificate of acknowledgement or attach one to the instrument.

✓ Answer key on Page 222

§ 1189. Certificate of acknowledgment; form; sufficiency of out of state acknowledgment; force and effect of acknowledgment under prior laws

(a) (1) Any certificate of acknowledgment taken within this state shall include a notice at the top of the certificate of acknowledgment in an enclosed box stating: "A notary public or other officer completing this certificate verifies only the identity of the individual who signed the document to which this certificate is attached, and not the truthfulness, accuracy, or validity of that document." This notice shall be legible.

(2) The physical format of the boxed notice at the top of the certificate of acknowledgment required pursuant to paragraph (3) is an example, for purposes of illustration and not limitation, of the physical format of a boxed notice fulfilling the requirements of paragraph

(3) A certificate of acknowledgment taken within this state shall be in the following form:

> A notary public or other officer completing this certificate verifies only the identity of the individual who signed the document to which this certificate is attached, and not the truthfulness, accuracy, or validity of that document.

State of California }
County of _____

On_____ before me, (here insert name and title of the officer), personally appeared

_____

_____

_____

_____, who proved to me on the basis of satisfactory evidence to be the person(s) whose name(s) is/are subscribed to the within instrument and acknowledged to me that he/she/they executed the same in his/her/their authorized capacity(ies), and that by his/her/their signature(s) on the instrument the person(s), or the entity upon behalf of which the person(s) acted, executed the instrument.

I certify under PENALTY OF PERJURY under the laws of the State of California that the foregoing paragraph is true and correct.

WITNESS my hand and official seal.

Signature _____ (Seal)

(4) A notary public who willfully states as true any material fact that he or she knows to be false shall be subject to a civil penalty not exceeding ten thousand dollars ($10,000). An action to impose a civil penalty under this subdivision may be brought by the Secretary of State in an administrative proceeding or any public prosecutor in superior court and shall be enforced as a civil judgment. A public prosecutor shall inform the secretary of any civil penalty imposed under this section.

(b) Any certificate of acknowledgment taken in another place shall be sufficient in this state if it is taken in accordance with the laws of the place where the acknowledgment is made.

(c) On documents to be filed in another state or jurisdiction of the United States, a California notary public may complete any acknowledgment form as may be required in that other state or jurisdiction on a document, provided the form does not require the notary to determine or certify that the signer holds a particular representative capacity or to make other determinations and certifications not allowed by California law.

(d) An acknowledgment provided prior to January 1, 1993, and conforming to applicable provisions of former Sections 1189, 1190, 1190a, 1190.1, 1191, and 1192, as repealed by Chapter 335 of the Statutes of 1990, shall have the same force and effect as if those sections had not been repealed.

SUMMARY

The certificate of acknowledgment must be in the format found in the official section above. In a certificate of acknowledgment, the notary public certifies that the signer personally appeared before the notary public in a certain county and on a certain date. The notary public certifies the signer and also certifies the signer acknowledged signing the document.

The certificate of acknowledgment must be fully completed when the notary public's signature and seal are added, and it is signed under penalty of perjury.

It is a criminal offense for a notary public to knowingly complete a certificate of acknowledgment containing statements the notary public knows to be false. The notary public may also be liable for civil penalties and administrative action subject to a civil penalty of not more than $10,000.00.

A notary public may complete a certificate of acknowledgment in a different format as required by another state or jurisdiction of the United States, as long as:

1. The document is to be filed in the other state or jurisdiction; and

2. As long as the document does not require the notary public to determine or certify that the signer holds a particular representative capacity or make any other

determinations and certifications about the document and/or signer which are not allowed by California law.

Any certificate of acknowledgment taken within this state must be in the following form: Reference the form found in the official section.

Note: A notary public cannot complete a certificate of acknowledgment on a document received via mail, delivery, or other means if the signer did not personally appear before the notary public, even if the signer is known by the notary public. Additionally, a notary public cannot sign and seal a document without the correct notarial wording.

TRUE OR FALSE?

93.   In a certificate of acknowledgment, the notary public is certifying that the signer proved their identity and acknowledged they signed the document.

✓ Answer key on Page 222

§ 1190. Certificate of acknowledgment as prima facie evidence; duly authorized person

The certificate of acknowledgment of an instrument executed on behalf of an incorporated or unincorporated entity by a duly authorized person in the form specified in Section 1189 shall be prima facie evidence that the instrument is the duly authorized act of the entity named in the instrument and shall be conclusive evidence thereof in favor of any good faith purchaser, lessee, or encumbrancer. "Duly authorized person," with respect to a domestic or foreign corporation, includes the president, vice president, secretary, and assistant secretary of the corporation.

SUMMARY

A certificate of acknowledgment for an instrument signed by a duly authorized person on behalf of an incorporated or unincorporated entity is presumed to be an authorized act of the entity if there is no reason for the notary to believe otherwise. If the entity is incorporated, this section further explains that an incorporated entity's president, vice-president, secretary, or assistant secretary are each considered a "duly authorized person".

TRUE OR FALSE?

94.   A notary public must be presented with proof of a signer's role as a duly authorized person for an entity before the person signs the document.

✓ Answer key on Page 222

§ 1193. Certificate of acknowledgment; authentication

Officers taking and certifying acknowledgments or proof of instruments for record, must authenticate their certificates by affixing thereto their signatures, followed by the names of their offices; also, their seals of office, if by the laws of the State or country where the acknowledgment or proof is taken, or by authority of which they are acting, they are required to have official seals.

SUMMARY

Officers, including notaries, who take and certify acknowledgments or proof of instruments for record, must authenticate their certificates of acknowledgment by signing the certificate and adding the names of their offices. If applicable, they must also affix their official seals to the instrument.

TRUE OR FALSE?

95.   If a notary public takes and certifies an acknowledgment, he/she must sign the certificate but does not need to affix their seal as long as the notary's name, county of business, and date of commission expiration is printed next to the notary's signature.

✓ Answer key on Page 222

§ 1195. Proof of execution; methods; certificate form

(a) Proof of the execution of an instrument, when not acknowledged, may be made by any of the following:
(1) By the party executing it, or either of them.
(2) By a subscribing witness.
(3) By other witnesses, in cases mentioned in Section 1198.
(b) (1) Proof of the execution of a power of attorney, grant deed, mortgage, deed of trust, quitclaim deed, security agreement, or any instrument affecting real property is not permitted pursuant to Section 27287 of the Government Code, though proof of the execution of a trustee's deed or deed of reconveyance is permitted.

(2) Proof of the execution for any instrument requiring a notary public to obtain a thumbprint from the party signing the document in the notary public's journal is not permitted.

(c) Any certificate for proof of execution taken within this state shall include a notice at the top of the certificate for proof of execution in an enclosed box stating: "A notary public or other officer completing this certificate verifies only the identity of the individual who signed the document to which this certificate is attached, and not the truthfulness, accuracy, or validity of that document." This notice shall be legible.

(d) The physical format of the boxed notice at the top of the certificate for proof of execution required pursuant to subdivision (e) is an example, for purposes of illustration and not limitation, of the physical format of a boxed notice fulfilling the requirements of subdivision (c).

(e) A certificate for proof of execution taken within this state shall be in the following form:

(3) A certificate of acknowledgment taken within this state shall be in the following form:

> A notary public or other officer completing this certificate verifies only the identity of the individual who signed the document to which this certificate is attached, and not the truthfulness, accuracy, or validity of that document.

State of California } ss.
County of _____

On (date), before me, _____ (name and title of officer), personally appeared _____ (name of subscribing witness), proved to me to be the person whose name is subscribed to the within instrument, as a witness thereto, on the oath of _____ (name of credible witness), a credible witness who is known to me and provided a satisfactory identifying document. _____ (name of subscribing witness), being by me duly sworn, said that he/she was present and saw/heard _____ (name[s] of principal[s]), the same person(s) described in and whose name(s) is/are subscribed to the within or attached instrument in his/her/their authorized capacity(ies) as (a) party (ies) thereto, execute or acknowledge executing the same, and that said affiant subscribed his/her name to the within or attached instrument as a witness at the request of _____ (name[s] of principal[s]).

WITNESS my hand and official seal.
Signature _____   (Seal)

SUMMARY

(a) Proof of the signing of an instrument after the fact, when it hasn't been acknowledged, may be made by any of the following:

(1) By the party(ies) who signed the instrument.
(2) By a subscribing witness.
(3) By other witnesses, in cases mentioned in Section 1198.
(b) (1) Proof of the signing of a power of attorney, grant deed, mortgage, deed of trust, quitclaim deed, security agreement, or any instrument affecting real property is not permitted. These instruments must be signed in front of the notary public. Proof of the execution of a trustee's deed or deed of reconveyance is permitted.

  (2) Proof of signing is not permitted for any instrument which requires a notary public to obtain a thumbprint from the signer in the notary public's journal.

(c) Any certificate for proof of execution taken within this state shall include a notice at the top of the certificate for proof of execution in an enclosed box stating: "A notary public or other officer completing this certificate verifies only the identity of the individual who signed the document to which this certificate is attached, and not the truthfulness, accuracy, or validity of that document". This notice shall be legible.

(d) The physical format of the boxed notice at the top of the certificate for proof of execution required pursuant to subdivision (e) is an example, for purposes of illustration and not limitation, of the physical format of a boxed notice fulfilling the requirements of subdivision (c).

(e) A certificate for proof of execution taken within this state shall be in the following form: Reference the form found in the official section.

TRUE OR FALSE?

96. Proof of the signing of an instrument cannot be done for a power of attorney.

✓ Answer key on Page 222

§ 1196. Subscribing witness; establishment of identity

A witness shall be proved to be a subscribing witness by the oath of a credible witness who provides the officer with any document satisfying the requirements of paragraph (3) or (4) of subdivision (b) of Section 1185.

SUMMARY

A witness who subscribes an instrument must have their identity proven by a separate credible witness. The credible witness must provide the notary with their oath and a valid document. Document requirements are stated in paragraph (3) or (4) of subdivision (b) of Section 1185.

TRUE OR FALSE?

97.   When a witness who subscribes a document for another person who is not present, the witness may prove their identity with a valid ID.

✓ Answer key on Page 222

§ 1197. Subscribing witness; items to be proved

The subscribing witness must prove that the person whose name is subscribed to the instrument as a party is the person described in it, and that such person executed it, and that the witness subscribed his name thereto as a witness.

SUMMARY

The subscribing witness must swear to the notary public that:

(a) The person whose name is signed on the instrument as a party is, in fact, the person described in the instrument; and

(b) That the person described in the instrument is the same person who signed it; and

(c) That the subscribing witness also subscribed their name to the instrument as a witness.

TRUE OR FALSE?

98.   A subscribing witness must only attest that the person who signed the instrument is the proper party, that he/she saw the person sign the instrument, and that their signature is also on the document as a subscribing witness.

✓ Answer key on Page 222

§ 1633.11. Notarization and signature under penalty of perjury requirements

If a law requires that a signature be notarized, the requirement is satisfied with respect to an electronic signature if an electronic record includes, in addition to the electronic signature to be notarized, the electronic signature of a notary public together with all other information required to be included in a notarization by other applicable law.

* * *

SUMMARY

An electronic signature may suffice as a legal, notarized signature if the electronic record attached to the signature includes the electronic signature of a notary public and all other information that would be required with a signature notarization on paper.

TRUE OR FALSE?

99. For a digital instrument to be considered validly signed by a party to the instrument, the party's electronic signature is enough if he copies the notary public in the CC line of the email.

✓ Answer key on Page 222

§ 1633.12. Retaining records; electronic satisfaction

(a) If a law requires that a record be retained, the requirement is satisfied by retaining an electronic record of the information in the record, if the electronic record reflects accurately the information set forth in the record at the time it was first generated in its final form as an electronic record or otherwise, and the electronic record remains accessible for later reference.

(b) A requirement to retain a record in accordance with subdivision (a) does not apply to any information the sole purpose of which is to enable the record to be sent, communicated, or received.

(c) A person may satisfy subdivision (a) by using the services of another person if the requirements of subdivision (a) are satisfied.

(d) If a law requires a record to be retained in its original form or provides consequences if the record is not retained in its original form, that law is satisfied by an electronic record retained in accordance with subdivision (a).

(e) If a law requires retention of a check, that requirement is satisfied by retention of an electronic record of the information on the front and back of the check in accordance with subdivision (a).

(f) A record retained as an electronic record in accordance with subdivision (a) satisfies a law requiring a person to retain a record for evidentiary, audit, or like purposes, unless a law enacted after the effective date of this title specifically prohibits the use of an electronic record for a specified purpose.

(g) This section does not preclude a governmental agency from specifying additional requirements for the retention of a record subject to the agency's jurisdiction.

SUMMARY

If a record is legally required to be retained, the requirement is satisfied by keeping an electronic record of the information as long as the electronic record accurately and fully reflects all data in the original record at the time it was generated and as long as the electronic record remains accessible for later reference. The requirement to retain a record does not apply to any information which was used solely to send, communicate, or receive the record.

A person may satisfy the requirements for retaining a record by using the services of another person and if a law requires a record to be retained in its original form, that law is fulfilled by keeping an electronic record as described above.

If the law requires the retention of a check, the requirement is satisfied by retaining an electronic record of the information on the front and back of the check. A record retained as an electronic record satisfies a law requiring a person to retain an original record for evidentiary, audit, or like purposes. This section does not, however, prevent a governmental agency from specifying its own additional criteria for retaining a record in that agency's jurisdiction.

TRUE OR FALSE?

100. If the law requires a party to retain an electronic copy of a scanned contract, the electronic record must also show the email addresses of the person who sent it, the person who received it, and anyone who may have been copied on the email.

✓ Answer key on Page 222

CODE OF CIVIL PRODEDURE

§ 12a. Computation of time; holidays; application of section

If the last day for the performance of any act provided or required by law to be performed within a specified period of time is a holiday, then that period is hereby extended to and including the next day that is not a holiday. For purposes of this section, "holiday" means all day on Saturdays, all holidays specified in Section 135 and, to the extent provided in Section 12b, all days that by terms of Section 12b are required to be considered as holidays. * * *

SUMMARY

If the last day of a deadline for any act required by law to be performed in a certain timeframe lands on a holiday, then that period is extended to the next day that is not a holiday. For this section, "holiday" means all day on Saturdays and all holidays specified in Section 135 and Section 12b must be considered as holidays.

EXAMPLE

A time computation for a deadline ends on a Saturday, therefore, the deadline is extended by a day to the next business day.

§ 1935. Subscribing witness defined

A subscribing witness is one who sees a writing executed or hears it acknowledged, and at the request of the party thereupon signs his name as a witness.

SUMMARY

A subscribing witness is a person who watches someone sign a written instrument or hears the signer verbally confirm that he/she signed it. The subscribing witness can sign their name as a witness if asked.

TRUE OR FALSE?

101. A person who witnesses their relative sign an instrument is known as a subscribing

witness.

✓ Answer key on Page 222

§ 2093. Officers authorized to administer oaths or affirmations

(a) A court, judge or clerk of a court, justice, notary public, and officer or person authorized to take testimony in an action or proceeding, or to decide upon evidence, has the power to administer oaths and affirmations.

(b) (1) A shorthand reporter certified pursuant to Article 3 (commencing with Section 8020) of Chapter 13 of Division 3 of the Business and Professions Code has the power to administer oaths and affirmations and may perform the duties of the deposition officer pursuant to Chapter 9 (commencing with Section 2025.010) of Title 4. The certified shorthand reporter is entitled to receive fees for services rendered during a deposition, including fees for deposition services, as specified in subdivision (c) of Section 8211 of the Government Code.

(2) This subdivision also applies to depositions taken by telephone or other remote electronic means as specified in Chapter 2 (commencing with Section 2017.010) and Chapter 9 (commencing with Section 2025.010) of Title 4.

(c) (1) A former judge or justice of a court of record in the state who retired or resigned from office may administer oaths and affirmations, if the former judge or justice requests and receives a certification from the Commission on Judicial Performance pursuant to paragraph (2).

(2) The Commission on Judicial Performance shall issue a certification enabling a former judge or justice to administer oaths and affirmations if the following conditions are satisfied:

(A) The former judge or justice was not removed from office; was not censured and barred from receiving an assignment, appointment, or reference of work from any California state court; did not retire or resign from office with an agreement with the commission that the former judge or justice would not receive an assignment, appointment or reference of work from any California state court; and, at the time of the former judge or justice's retirement, resignation, or request for certification, a formal disciplinary proceeding was not pending or was resolved on the merits in the judge or justice's favor after his or her retirement or resignation and before the request for certification.

(B) A medical certification provided to the commission by the former judge or justice pursuant to paragraph (3) establishes one of the following:

(i) The former judge or justice does not have a medical condition that would impair his or her ability to administer oaths or affirmations.

(ii) The former judge or justice has a medical condition that may impair his or her ability to administer oaths and affirmations, but the condition does not impair his or her ability at the present time.

(3) The Commission on Judicial Performance may require an applicant to obtain a medical certification in order to receive or renew a certification to administer oaths and affirmations if, at the time of resignation or retirement, there is evidence in a disability application file or in a disciplinary investigation file of possible cognitive impairment affecting the judge or justice, or if the former judge or justice previously received a two-year certification to administer oaths and affirmations from the commission. The commission shall supply the required forms to an applicant upon request.

(4) If an applicant's medical certification indicates that the applicant has a medical condition that may impair his or her ability to administer oaths and affirmations, but the condition does not impair his or her ability at the time the medical certification is submitted with the application, the Commission on Judicial Performance shall issue a certification to administer oaths and affirmations pursuant to paragraph (2), but the certification is only valid for a period of two years from the date of issuance.

(5) Notwithstanding paragraph (1), a former judge or justice of a court of record who received a certification to administer oaths and affirmations from the Commission on Judicial Performance prior to January 1, 2018, may continue to administer oaths and affirmations until the expiration of the certification, at which time he or she may reapply for certification pursuant to paragraph (2).

(6) The Commission on Judicial Performance may charge a regulatory fee not to exceed fifteen dollars ($15) for each certification application submitted pursuant to this subdivision to cover its costs, including costs to review a medical certification.

(d) A rule or regulation regarding the confidentiality of proceedings of the Commission on Judicial Performance does not prohibit the commission from issuing a certificate as provided for in this section.

(e) The administration of an oath or affirmation pursuant to this section without pay does not violate Section 75060.6 of the Government Code.

* * *

SUMMARY

A court, judge or clerk of a court, justice, notary public, and officer or person authorized to take testimony in an action or proceeding, or to decide upon evidence, has the power to administer oaths and affirmations.

A shorthand reporter certified pursuant to the appropriate regulations has the power to administer oaths and affirmations and may also perform the duties of the deposition officer. The certified shorthand reporter is entitled to receive fees for services rendered during a deposition, including fees for deposition.

A former judge or justice of a court of record in the state who retired or resigned from office may administer oaths and affirmations, if the former judge or justice requests and receives a certification from the Commission on Judicial Performance. The Commission on Judicial Performance establishes all rules, regulations, and guidelines necessary to determine the fitness and suitability of former judges and justices to administer oaths and affirmations.

TRUE OR FALSE?

102. A former judge or justice of a court who resigned or retired and wishes to be certified to administer oaths and affirmations must first be approved and certified by the Commission on Judicial Performance.

✓ Answer key on Page 222

§ 2094. Oath to witness; form

An oath, affirmation, or declaration in an action or a proceeding, may be administered by obtaining an affirmative response to one of the following questions:
"Do you solemnly state that the evidence you shall give in this issue (or matter) shall be the truth, the whole truth, and nothing but the truth, so help you God?"
"Do you solemnly state, under penalty of perjury, that the evidence that you shall give in this issue (or matter) shall be the truth, the whole truth, and nothing but the truth?"
* * *

SUMMARY

During any action or proceeding, a notary public can give an oath, affirmation, or declaration by getting an affirmative response ("Yes") to one of the following questions:

"Do you solemnly state that the evidence you shall give in this issue (or matter) shall be the truth, the whole truth, and nothing but the truth, so help you God?"; or

"Do you solemnly state, under penalty of perjury, that the evidence that you shall give in this issue (or matter) shall be the truth, the whole truth, and nothing but the truth?"
* * *

TRUE OR FALSE?

103. When an oath is administered, the witness must raise their right hand.

✓ Answer key on Page 222

ELECTIONS CODE

§ 8080. Fee for verification

No fee or charge shall be made or collected by any officer for verifying any nomination document or circulator's affidavit.

SUMMARY

An officer cannot charge or collect a fee for verifying a nomination document or circulator's affidavit.

TRUE OR FALSE?

104. A notary public is prohibited from charging a fee to verify a nomination document or circulator's affidavit unless the notary is employed by a government agency who requires a notary to collect the fee and remit it to the government agency.

✓ Answer key on Page 222

COMMERCIAL CODE

§ 3505. Protest; Noting for Protest

* * *

(b) A protest is a certificate of dishonor made by a United States consul or vice consul, or a notary public during the course and scope of employment with a financial institution or other person authorized to administer oaths by the laws of any other state, government, or country in the place where dishonor occurs. It may be made upon information satisfactory to that person. The protest shall identify the instrument and certify either that presentment has been made or, if not made, the reason why it was not made, and that the instrument has been dishonored by nonacceptance or nonpayment. The protest may also certify that notice of dishonor has been given to some or all parties.

SUMMARY

A protest is a certificate declaring dishonor, which is a default in payment on a promissory note. A protest can be made by:
- A notary public employed by a financial institution;
- A U.S. consul;
- A U.S. vice consul; or
- A person authorized to certify dishonor by the law of the place where dishonor occurs.

The protest must:
1. Identify the instrument;
2. Mention that the instrument was dishonored by nonacceptance or by nonpayment; and
3. a. Certify that presentment was made; or
   b. The reason presentment was not made;

Evidence must be presented to the person the protest was made to. It is up to that person's discretion to decide whether or not the evidence presented is satisfactory.

The protest may also certify that it has been given to all parties or to specified parties.

TRUE OR FALSE?

105. A notary public employed by a financial institution may make a protest on a financial

instrument after dishonor has occurred no matter the information provided.

✓ Answer key on Page 222

PROBATE CODE

§ 4307. Certified copies of power of attorney

(a) A copy of a power of attorney certified under this section has the same force and effect as the original power of attorney.

(b) A copy of a power of attorney may be certified by any of the following:

(1) An attorney authorized to practice law in this state.

(2) A notary public in this state.

(3) An official of a state or of a political subdivision who is authorized to make certifications.

(c) The certification shall state that the certifying person has examined the original power of attorney and the copy and that the copy is a true and correct copy of the original power of attorney.

(d) Nothing in this section is intended to create an implication that a third person may be liable for acting in good faith reliance on a copy of a power of attorney that has not been certified under this section.

SUMMARY

A copy of a power of attorney certified under this section has the same force and effect as the original power of attorney. A copy of a power of attorney may be certified by an attorney authorized to practice law in this state, a notary public in this state, or an official of a state or political division who is authorized to make certifications. The certification must state the certifying person has examined the original power of attorney and the copy and that the copy is a true and correct copy of the original power of attorney.

TRUE OR FALSE?

106. To certify a copy of a power of attorney, the certifying official must have the original power of attorney to be able to inspect and compare it to the copy before certifying.

✓ Answer key on Page 222

PENAL CODE

§ 17. Felony; misdemeanor; infraction; classification of offenses

(a) A felony is a crime that is punishable with death, by imprisonment in the state prison, or notwithstanding any other provision of law, by imprisonment in a county jail under the provisions of subdivision (h) of Section 1170. Every other crime or public offense is a misdemeanor except those offenses that are classified as infractions. * * *

SUMMARY

A felony is a crime punishable with death, imprisonment in state prison, or imprisonment in county jail under certain circumstances. Every other crime or offense is classified as a misdemeanor except offenses which are called infractions. * * *

TRUE OR FALSE?

107. Punishment for a misdemeanor may include incarceration for a certain period in municipal jail.

✓ Answer key on Page 222

§ 115.5. Filing false or forged documents relating to single-family residences; punishment; false statement to notary public

(a) Every person who files any false or forged document or instrument with the county recorder which affects title to, places an encumbrance on, or places an interest secured by a mortgage or deed of trust on, real property consisting of a single-family residence containing not more than four dwelling units, with knowledge that the document is false or forged, is punishable, in addition to any other punishment, by a fine not exceeding seventy-five thousand dollars ($75,000).

(b) Every person who makes a false sworn statement to a notary public, with knowledge that the statement is false, to induce the notary public to perform an improper notarial act on an instrument or document affecting title to, or placing an encumbrance on, real property consisting of a single-family residence containing not more than four dwelling units is guilty of a felony.

SUMMARY

Any person who knowingly files any false or forged instrument with the county recorder which affects the title to, or creates a debt, lien, or mortgage obligation on real property consisting of a single-family residence is punishable, in addition to any other punishment, by a fine not exceeding $75,000.00. Any person who knowingly makes a false sworn statement to a notary public to induce the notary public to perform an improper notarial act on an instrument or document affecting title to, or placing an encumbrance on, real property consisting of a single-family residence containing not more than four dwelling units is guilty of a felony.

TRUE OR FALSE?

108. Knowingly defrauding or misleading a notary public to induce the notary to perform an improper notarial act affecting the title of and/or encumbrances on any real property with a single-family home on it is guilty of a felony.

✓ Answer key on Page 222

§ 118. Perjury defined; evidence necessary to support conviction

(a) Every person who, having taken an oath that he or she will testify, declare, depose, or certify truly before any competent tribunal, officer, or person, in any of the cases in which the oath may by law of the State of California be administered, willfully and contrary to the oath, states as true any material matter which he or she knows to be false, and every person who testifies, declares, deposes, or certifies under penalty of perjury in any of the cases in which the testimony, declarations, depositions, or certification is permitted by law of the State of California under penalty of perjury and willfully states as true any material matter which he or she knows to be false, is guilty of perjury. This subdivision is applicable whether the statement, or the testimony, declaration, deposition, or certification is made or subscribed within or without the State of California.

(b) No person shall be convicted of perjury where proof of falsity rests solely upon contradiction by testimony of a single person other than the defendant. Proof of falsity may be established by direct or indirect evidence.

SUMMARY

A person is guilty of perjury if he/she is placed under oath and swears to testify or speak truthfully under penalty of perjury and states any material matter as:

1. True and knows that it is false; and/or

2. False and knows that it is true

No person shall be convicted of perjury where proof of truthfulness or falsehood rests solely upon contradicting testimony from another person other than the defendant.

TRUE OR FALSE?

109. A person who lies while under oath after having sworn to tell the truth, is guilty of perjury but that person will not be convicted if the only proof of their perjury is the statement of someone else, creating a "he said/she said" situation.

✓ Answer key on Page 222

§ 126. Punishment

Perjury is punishable by imprisonment pursuant to subdivision (h) of Section 1170 for two, three or four years.

SUMMARY

Perjury is punishable by imprisonment for two, three or four years.

§ 470. Forgery; signatures or seals; corruption of records

* * *
(b) Every person who, with the intent to defraud, counterfeits or forges the seal or handwriting of another is guilty of forgery.
* * *
(d) Every person who, with the intent to defraud, falsely makes, alters, forges, or counterfeits, utters, publishes, passes or attempts or offers to pass, as true and genuine, any of the following items, knowing the same to be false, altered, forged, or counterfeited, is guilty of forgery:
… or falsifies the acknowledgment of any notary public, or any notary public who issues an acknowledgment knowing it to be false; or any matter described in subdivision (b).
* * *

SUMMARY

Anyone who intentionally commits fraud by counterfeiting or forging the seal or handwriting of another person is guilty of forgery. Anyone who intentionally commits fraud by forging the acknowledgment of any notary public is guilty of forgery. And any notary public who issues an acknowledgment knowing it is false is also guilty of forgery.

TRUE OR FALSE?

110. Anyone who copies someone else's signature, mark, or seal is guilty of forgery, even if the other person authorized or requested the first person to sign for them.

✓ Answer key on Page 222

§ 473. Forgery; punishment

(a) Forgery is punishable by imprisonment in a county jail for not more than one year, or by imprisonment pursuant to subdivision (h) of Section 1170.

SUMMARY

(a) Forgery is punishable by imprisonment in a county jail for not more than one year, or by imprisonment pursuant to subdivision (h) of Section 1170.

§ 830.3. Peace officers; employing agencies; authority

The following persons are peace officers whose authority extends to any place in the state for the purpose of performing their primary duty or when making an arrest pursuant to Section 836 as to any public offense with respect to which there is immediate danger to person or property, or of the escape of the perpetrator of that offense, or pursuant to Section 8597 or 8598 of the Government Code. * * *
(o) Investigators of the office of the Secretary of State designated by the Secretary of State, provided that the primary duty of these peace officers shall be the enforcement of the law as prescribed in Chapter 3 (commencing with Section 8200) of Division 1 of Title 2 of, and Section 12172.5 of, the Government Code. * * *

SUMMARY

Investigators of the office of the Secretary of State designated by the Secretary of State are peace officers whose authority extends anywhere in the state for the purpose of performing their primary duty.

BUSINESS AND PROFESSIONAL CODE

§ 22449. Deferred Action for Childhood Arrivals program; price gouging; penalties

(a) Immigration consultants, attorneys, notaries public, and organizations accredited by the United States Board of Immigration Appeals shall be the only individuals authorized to charge clients or prospective clients fees for providing consultations, legal advice, or notary public services, respectively, associated with filing an application under the federal Deferred Action for Childhood Arrivals program announced by the United States Secretary of Homeland Security on June 15, 2012.

(b) (1) Immigration consultants, attorneys, notaries public, and organizations accredited by the United States Board of Immigration Appeals shall be prohibited from participating in practices that amount to price gouging when a client or prospective client solicits services associated with filing an application for deferred action for childhood arrivals as described in subdivision (a).

(2) For the purposes of this section, "price gouging" means any practice that has the effect of pressuring the client or prospective client to purchase services immediately because purchasing them at a later time will result in the client or prospective client paying a higher price for the same services.

(c) (1) In addition to the civil and criminal penalties described in Section 22445, a violation of this section by an attorney shall be cause for discipline by the State Bar pursuant to Chapter 4 (commencing with Section 6000) of Division 3.

(2) In addition to the civil and criminal penalties described in Section 22445, a violation of this section by a notary public shall be cause for the revocation or suspension of his or her commission as a notary public by the Secretary of State and the application of any other applicable penalties pursuant to Chapter 3 (commencing with Section 8200) of Division 1 of Title 2 of the Government Code.

SUMMARY

Immigration consultants, attorneys, notaries public, and organizations accredited by the United States Board of Immigration Appeals shall be the only individuals authorized to charge clients or prospective clients fees for providing consultations, legal advice, or notary public services. They are also prohibited from participating in practices that amount to price gouging when a client or prospective client solicits services associated with filing an application for deferred action for childhood arrivals. "Price gouging" means any practice that has the effect of pressuring the client or prospective client to purchase services immediately because purchasing them at a later time will result in the client or prospective client paying a higher price for the same services.

In addition to the civil and criminal penalties described in Section 22445, a violation of this section by a notary public shall be cause for the revocation or suspension of their commission by the Secretary of State and the imposition of any other applicable penalties of the Government Code.

TRUE OR FALSE?

111. A notary public is not allowed to charge a fee for notarial services if the client or prospective client needs their signature verified and notarized on immigration-related documents.

✓ Answer key on Page 222

DEFINITIONS AND GENERAL TERMS

Acknowledgment

A formal declaration made before an officer (i.e. notary public) by a person who has executed a written instrument as his free act and deed.

A notary public should not take an acknowledgment if he has an interest in the legal instrument.

A notary public who makes a false certificate is guilty of forgery in the second degree. It is punishable by imprisonment for a term of not exceeding 7 years.

A notary public taking acknowledgments over the telephone is guilty of a misdemeanor.

Affiant

The person who swears to an affidavit.

Affidavit

A sworn statement signed by the person swearing by it. It is sworn personally before a notary public or other officer who has the authority to administer an oath.

An affidavit is an ex parte statement.

Affirmation

Someone who declines to take an oath for religious, ethical, or other reasons. Instead of taking an oath, the person may affirm that certain statements are true. It is equivalent to an oath and is just as binding.

Attest

To be present and subscribe as a witness to the execution of a written instrument, at the request of the person who makes it.

Authentication (Notarial)

A document signed by a notary public that is authenticated by a county clerk. This authenticates/verifies the authority of the notary public. Also called county clerk's certificate.

Certified Copy

A signed and certified public record meant to certify that it is the original copy. Only public officials that have the original copy can perform the certification. A notary public cannot issue certified copies.

Contract

An agreement between parties for a legal consideration.

Deed of Reconveyance

A legal document that serves as proof of a deed (or title) which creates, transfers, assigns, or surrenders any estate or interest in real property.

Deposition

A witness's sworn out-of-court testimony under oath or by affirmation, before an authorized official. It is used at the trial or hearing.

Escrow

An instrument that is put into the custody of a third-party to be held until the occurrence of an event.

Executor

A person named in a will to carry out the requirements of the will.

Felony

A crime punishable by death or imprisonment in a state prison.

Judgment

A decision of a court regarding the rights and liabilities of parties in a legal action or proceeding.

Jurat

The clause at the end of the document stating the date, place, and name of the officer (notary public) certifies that it was sworn to before him.

The following is generally used as a form of jurat:

"Sworn to before me this .... day of ...., 20 ......"

Lease

A contract made for a consideration (i.e. rent) in which the owner of property (real estate, car, etc.) allows use of the property for a specified period of time (term).

Lien

The right to retain the possession of another person's property until the owner fulfills a legal duty to the person holding the property, such as a satisfying a debt.

Litigation

The act of carrying on a lawsuit.

Misdemeanor

Any crime other than a felony.

Mortgage On Real Property

A legal document that creates a lien on real estate as security until a debt has been satisfied.

Notary Public

A public officer who can perform many duties such as:

- Executes acknowledgments of deeds
- Administer oaths and affirmations the truthfulness of statements on documents
- Take affidavits declarations

Oath

A declaration made by the person taking it that his statements are true to his knowledge. It must be taken before an authorized person (notary public).

An oath must be administered as required by law personally in front of a notary public and cannot be administered over the telephone.

The person taking the oath must say "I do" or something similar in meaning.

A corporation or a partnership cannot take an oath.

A notary public cannot administer an oath to himself.

Plaintiff

A person or group who initiates a lawsuit against another party.

Power of Attorney

A legal document giving one person the power to act for another person.

Proof

A formal declaration made by a subscribing witness usually stating that he witnessed the signature of the signer of the document.

Protest

A formal declaration made by a notary public declaring a default in payment on a promissory note.

Statute

A law established by an act of the Legislature.

Swear

To take an oath.

Will

An instrument by which a person makes a disposition of his property to take effect after death.

NOTARY PUBLIC EXAM

EXAM INFORMATION

The allotted time for the exam is 1-hour. There are 45 multiple-choice questions on the exam but will be a scored based on 40 questions. The 5 non-scored questions do not count against the applicant's exam score and is only included to collect information for next year's exam. A scaled score of at least 70% is required to pass the exam. A scaled score is a conversion of the applicant's raw score on one exam form to a common scale used for all the exam scores.

Exam results will be emailed or mailed once the results are available; typically, within 15-20 business days. Applicant's that pass the exam will have their applications forwarded to the Secretary of State's office for processing. From there, applicant's will be instructed to submit fingerprints via Live Scan. Live Scan is a background check program by the California Department of Justice and FBI.

Applicant's not passing the exam will be emailed or mailed a fail notice. Applicants who fail the exam may apply and test again, but may not test more than once a calendar month.

TEST-TAKING STRATEGIES

MAKE PREDICTIONS

Your mind is typically the most focused immediately after you have read the question. Try predicting the answer right before reading the answer choices. This technique is useful on questions that test objective factual knowledge. By predicting the answer before reading the available choices, you eliminate the possibility that you will be distracted or led astray by an incorrect answer choice. Scan the answers to see if your prediction is one of the choices. If it is, you can be quite confident that you have the right answer. You will feel more confident in selection if you read the question, predict the answer, and then find your prediction among the answer choices. After using this strategy, be sure to still read all of the answer choices carefully and completely.

ANSWER THE QUESTION

Test authors create some excellent answer choices that are wrong. Don't pick an answer just because it sounds right or you believe it to be true. It MUST answer the question. Don't choose an answer that is factually true but is an incorrect choice because it does not answer the question. Once you've made your selection, go back and check it against the question and make sure you didn't misread the question, and that your choice does answer the question posed. For instance, a test author might turn the question into a negative redirect the focus of the question right at the end. Avoid falling into these traps by reading the answer choices carefully.

PROCESS OF ELIMINATION

The first step in answering long and complicated questions is to make sure you understand what the question is asking. Sometimes it helps to rephrase the question into a statement, or a simpler question. Once you're sure you know what the question is asking, you'll want to begin by eliminating any answer choices that are clearly wrong. Even if doing so only eliminates one out of four or five answer choices, you've still improved your odds of choosing the correct answer choice.

DIFFICULT QUESTIONS

As much as you have prepared to take the test, it is likely that you will come across a few questions for which you simply don't know the answer. In this situation, don't waste too much time on questions that appear too hard or difficult. Follow the process of elimination stated above to try to identify any obviously incorrect answers and guess at the remaining answer choices before giving up. Carefully think about each possible choice independently from the other choices. Ask yourself if it is possible that it could be the correct answer. When going through each choice this way, you are often able to discover things you might have overlooked. After eliminating obviously wrong answers, make a selection and move on to the next question.

CONFUSING ANSWER CHOICES

There may be a tendency to focus on answer choices that are easiest to comprehend. Many people gravitate to these answer choices because they require less concentration. This is a mistake. Many people fall into this trap designed by test authors. It may be difficult to identify so read through each answer choice carefully. Give these types of questions extra attention. When you come across an answer choice that is confusing, you should give it extra attention. Try to make sense of it. If it is still confusing, set it aside and examine the remaining choices. If you are confident that another answer choice is the correct answer, you can leave the confusing answer choice aside. Otherwise, try rephrasing the confusing answer choice to make sense of it in the context of the question.

DIFFICULT WORDS

Don't choose an answer choice just because it is the only one word you recognize. If you only recognize the words in one answer choice and not the rest, make sure it is correct and really answers the question before you choose it. If you can eliminate it, then you increase your chances of getting the right answer even if you have to guess. Try dissecting difficult words. Notice prefixes and suffixes and words like *may, can, often, rarely*, etc. An answer choice may be wrong because it doesn't contain these words but has words like *exactly* and *never*, which leaves no room for exception.

SWITCHBACK WORDS

Be careful for switchback words such as *but, although,* and *nevertheless*. They will alter the nature of the question and are there to throw you off. Negative words, such as *not* or *except* will subtly reverse the meaning of a question. This trap can easily lead you astray if you are not paying attention to each word in the question. For example, missing the reversal word in the question "Which of the following is not…?," will cause you to answer incorrectly. You might be so confident that you will not reread the question and move on without realizing the original error. A good strategy is to underline or highlight each switchback and negative word in the question to keep track of them easily. Pay close attention to each and every word to avoid this trick.

PRACTICE TESTS

TAKING THE PRACTICE TEST

The practice tests will help you most if you take it under conditions as close as possible to those of the actual test.

Each practice exam consists of 40 questions since the official exam has a total of 45 questions but there are 5 non-scored items.

- **Set aside 1 hour of uninterrupted time.**
  That way you can complete the entire test in one sitting.

- **Sit at a desk or table cleared of any other papers, books, and electronic devices.**
  You won't be able to take a dictionary, books, notes, scratch paper, phone, or laptop into the test room.

- **Record your answers on paper, then score your test.**
  Use the answer sheet when completing a practice test to simulate the real testing environment. After completing the practice test, you can score the test yourself. *Note:* The passing grade is 70%, meaning you must get at least 28 answers correct!

PRACTICE TEST 1: ANSWER SHEET

1. Ⓐ Ⓑ Ⓒ Ⓓ   11. Ⓐ Ⓑ Ⓒ Ⓓ   21. Ⓐ Ⓑ Ⓒ Ⓓ   31. Ⓐ Ⓑ Ⓒ Ⓓ

2. Ⓐ Ⓑ Ⓒ Ⓓ   12. Ⓐ Ⓑ Ⓒ Ⓓ   22. Ⓐ Ⓑ Ⓒ Ⓓ   32. Ⓐ Ⓑ Ⓒ Ⓓ

3. Ⓐ Ⓑ Ⓒ Ⓓ   13. Ⓐ Ⓑ Ⓒ Ⓓ   23. Ⓐ Ⓑ Ⓒ Ⓓ   33. Ⓐ Ⓑ Ⓒ Ⓓ

4. Ⓐ Ⓑ Ⓒ Ⓓ   14. Ⓐ Ⓑ Ⓒ Ⓓ   24. Ⓐ Ⓑ Ⓒ Ⓓ   34. Ⓐ Ⓑ Ⓒ Ⓓ

5. Ⓐ Ⓑ Ⓒ Ⓓ   15. Ⓐ Ⓑ Ⓒ Ⓓ   25. Ⓐ Ⓑ Ⓒ Ⓓ   35. Ⓐ Ⓑ Ⓒ Ⓓ

6. Ⓐ Ⓑ Ⓒ Ⓓ   16. Ⓐ Ⓑ Ⓒ Ⓓ   26. Ⓐ Ⓑ Ⓒ Ⓓ   36. Ⓐ Ⓑ Ⓒ Ⓓ

7. Ⓐ Ⓑ Ⓒ Ⓓ   17. Ⓐ Ⓑ Ⓒ Ⓓ   27. Ⓐ Ⓑ Ⓒ Ⓓ   37. Ⓐ Ⓑ Ⓒ Ⓓ

8. Ⓐ Ⓑ Ⓒ Ⓓ   18. Ⓐ Ⓑ Ⓒ Ⓓ   28. Ⓐ Ⓑ Ⓒ Ⓓ   38. Ⓐ Ⓑ Ⓒ Ⓓ

9. Ⓐ Ⓑ Ⓒ Ⓓ   19. Ⓐ Ⓑ Ⓒ Ⓓ   29. Ⓐ Ⓑ Ⓒ Ⓓ   39. Ⓐ Ⓑ Ⓒ Ⓓ

10. Ⓐ Ⓑ Ⓒ Ⓓ   20. Ⓐ Ⓑ Ⓒ Ⓓ   30. Ⓐ Ⓑ Ⓒ Ⓓ   40. Ⓐ Ⓑ Ⓒ Ⓓ

PRACTICE TEST 1 QUESTIONS

1. What action can the Secretary of State take against a notary public who fails to secure their seal properly?

   A. The Secretary of State can issue a warning to the notary public
   B. The Secretary of State can suspend the commission held by the notary public
   C. The Secretary of State can revoke the commission held by the notary public
   D. The Secretary of State cannot take any action against the notary public

2. A notary does not have a direct financial or beneficial interest in a transaction if the notary:

   A. Is individually named as a principal in a power of attorney
   B. Is individually named as a real estate trustor
   C. Is acting as the agent for a beneficiary
   D. Is notarizing the signature of a tenant renting an apartment from the notary public

3. Which of the following is true regarding notary publics and electronic notarizations?

   A. Electronic notarizations can be performed on any type of document
   B. Electronic notarizations do not require the use of a seal

   C. A physical appearance before the notary public is required for acknowledgments or jurats
   D. None of the above

4. Which form requires the notary public to administer an oath or affirmation to the affiant asking if they swear (or affirm) the instrument to be true and accurate?

   A. A jurat
   B. A certificate of acknowledgment
   C. A deposition
   D. A government database index

5. Any officer, including notaries public, who take and certify an acknowledgment or proof of instrument for record must authenticate their certificates of acknowledgment with:

   A. Their printed name
   B. The address of their primary place of business
   C. Their official seal, if one is used for their office
   D. Their commission number

6. How long does a notary public have to respond to a written request from the Secretary of State by certified mail for information on official acts performed by the notary public?

   A. 15 business days
   B. 30 days

C. Certified mail is not an authorized means of delivery

D. 24 hours

7. Any moneys received by the Secretary of State pursuant to Section 8214.15.d. of the Government Code shall be used to defray its costs incurred for:

A. Processing notary public applications and postage

B. Review and approval of notary study courses proposed by vendors

C. Investigating/pursuing commissioning and monetary remedies for violations of the notary public laws

D. Maintaining an up to date California Notary Handbook and making it available to the public at all times

8. The only persons qualified to be appointed and commissioned as notaries public on military reservations are:

A. Federal civil service employees currently working at the military reserve where they will be appointed

B. Federal civil service employees who have worked at least one year at the military reserve where they will be appointed

C. Federal civil service employees who formerly worked at the military reserve where they will be appointed

D. Federal civil service employees currently both working and residing at the military reserve where they will be appointed

9. A person who falsely claims to be a notary public during a transaction involving a deed of trust transfer of ownership may be:

A. Charged with a felony

B. Charged with a misdemeanor

C. Have their driver's license suspended

D. Required to take a notary public education course, apply for, and become commissioned as a notary public so that he/she may notarize the document a second time to make it valid

10. For the purposes of calculating any deadline in which a notary must act, or be acted upon, the first day is:

A. Counted, with the last day also counted

B. Not counted, with the last day counted unless it's Christmas Day

C. Not counted, with the last day not counted at any time of year

D. Counted, with the last day counted unless it's Christmas Day

11. What is the minimum age to be a notary public?

A. 21 years old

B. Whatever age the bonding company requires (various)

C. 18 years old

D. 25 years old, which may be waived to allow 21-year-old applicants with approval from the Secretary of State

12. What does the term "satisfactory evidence" mean?

   A. The absence of information or evidence which suggests the signer is an imposter
   B. The signer is personally known to the witness
   C. Both of the above
   D. None of the above

13. Which of the following items are the requirements for an official self-inking seal of a notary public?

   A. Black ink only
   B. Have a dotted border
   C. Both of the above
   D. None of the above

14. If a canceled check is discovered to be evidence of a criminal act, the canceled check shall be:

   A. The original paper document, retrieved from the bank's archives to prove there was no tampering with the document
   B. Retained as proof and considered a valid record of the canceled check if the information on the front and back of the check is stored electronically
   C. Inadmissible as an electronic record unless all parties to the check swear under oath it is a true and correct copy of the instrument
   D. Inadmissible as an electronic record unless the original paper document is attached and available for inspection

15. What should a notary public do with their official seal after their commission has expired, terminated, or resigned by the notary public?

   A. If employed by a government entity, the notary public must surrender the official seal and all fees collected to the government entity employer
   B. Throw it away
   C. Deliver it to the Secretary of State via certified mail or other delivery method which provides a receipt
   D. Destroy or deface it

16. The only officer authorized to collect a fee or charge for verifying a nomination or circulator's affidavit is:

   A. A notary public
   B. A county clerk
   C. A Board of Elections clerk
   D. None of the above

17. The only document a notary public may certify as a true and correct copy of the original is:

   A. A birth certificate
   B. A power of attorney
   C. A marriage license
   D. A business license

18. Willful failure to notify the Secretary of State of a change of address of the notary public's principal place of business is punishable by a fine in the amount of:

   A. No more than $500

B. No less than $500

C. $1,500

D. $250

19. Perjury is punishable by imprisonment for what periods of time?

   A. 6 months, 18 months, or 2 years

   B. 2 years, 3 years, or 4 years

   C. 3 years, 4 years, or 5 years

   D. 4 years, 5 years, or 6 years

20. The agency that issues certificates of authorization is the:

   A. Court Commissioner

   B. Department of Motor Vehicles

   C. Secretary of State

   D. Department of Justice

21. When a court issues a temporary or permanent injunction to stop someone from prohibited practices, the court may:

   A. Order the person to reimburse the Secretary of State for the costs of the investigation and injunction process

   B. Place the person on house arrest

   C. Surrender their driver's license and/or passport

   D. None of the above

22. The size of the stamp could be:

   A. 2 inch in diameter

   B. 1 inch in width by 2 ½ inches in length

   C. 2 ½ inches in width by 4 inches in length

D. A & B

23. A certificate of acknowledgment is signed by:

   A. Notary public

   B. Secretary of State

   C. Client

   D. Lender

24. Notaries can withhold services:

   A. When their employer limits services to transactions related to the employer's business

   B. When a document is incomplete

   C. When they believe someone does not understand what they are signing

   D. All of the above

25. Which of the following is true regarding a notarizing incomplete documents?

   A. A notary public must notarize all documents presented to them, even if they are incomplete

   B. A notary public may notarize incomplete documents if they have been approved by a government agency

   C. A notary public must refuse to notarize a document if they know it to be incomplete

   D. A notary public may only refuse to notarize a document if it is explicitly stated to be incomplete

26. Suppose Alexa who is named as grantee on a Grant Deed that is to be

notarized agrees to be a Credible Witness for her friend, Kevin, named as Grantor on a different Grant Deed. Which following statement is true?

A. Alexa may not be used as a credible witness for Kevin since she is a friend of Kevin

B. Alexa may be used as a credible witness for Kevin in this case

C. Credible Witnesses may never be used for Quitclaim Deeds, Grant Deeds, Deeds of Trust, Security Agreements, or Mortgage Agreements

D. The notary should contact the originator of the document requiring Kevin's signature prior to using Alexa as a Credible Witness

27. Which of the following statements is true about the certificate of acknowledgment of an instrument executed on behalf of an incorporated or unincorporated entity?

A. The certificate is not necessary if the instrument is executed by an authorized person

B. The certificate is only necessary if the instrument is executed by a foreign corporation

C. The certificate serves as prima facie evidence that the instrument is the duly authorized act of the entity named in the instrument

D. The certificate is only valid if executed by the president of the corporation

28. Brenda has applied for a job that requires a background check. As part of the application process, she is asked to submit her fingerprints and related information to the Department of Justice. The Department of Justice is trying to obtain information on the applicant's:

A. Criminal history
B. Credit history
C. Employment history
D. Educational background

29. What must a subscribing witness prove under oath?

A. The identity of the person who signed the document

B. The notary public's identity and qualifications

C. That the subscribing witness personally knows the notary public

D. That the notary public personally knows a credible witness

30. What is the required notice for non-attorney notary public advertising in another language?

A. Prescribed notice in English and the other language

B. Legal advice about immigration or any other legal matters

C. Notice that the notary public is not an attorney

D. List of fees in English and the other language

31. If a notary public resigns their commission and refuses to deliver all

notarial records and papers to the county clerk where their current oath and bond are filed, the notary public is guilty of which of the following?

A. An administrative violation
B. A misdemeanor
C. A felony
D. Obstruction of justice

32. Which of the following statements is true regarding the fee a notary public can charge for their services?

A. A notary public may charge less than the maximum fee prescribed by law
B. A notary public may charge any amount they wish for their services
C. A notary public is prohibited from charging any fee for their services
D. A notary public is required to charge the maximum fee prescribed by law

33. A notary public may charge no more than the following amount to notarize a person's pension application:

A. $5
B. $15
C. None
D. $7

34. Which form requires the following notice to be attached at the top of the form in an enclosed box: "A notary public or other officer completing this certificate verifies only the identity of the individual who signed the document to which this certificate is

attached, and not the truthfulness, accuracy, or validity of that document."

A. A certificate of acknowledgment
B. A certificate of authorization
C. A power of attorney document
D. A jurat

35. In what circumstances does the duty of a notary public to demand acceptance and payment of foreign and inland bills of exchange, or promissory notes, apply?

A. Only when the notary public is employed by a financial institution
B. Only when the notary public is not employed by a financial institution
C. Regardless of whether the notary public is employed by a financial institution
D. Only when the notary public is employed by a government agency

36. If a notary public is convicted of a felony, the court shall:

A. Revoke the notary public's commission
B. Require the notary public to hand over their official seal to the court so the court can forward it to the Secretary of State
C. Require the notary public to destroy or disfigure their official seal before relinquishing it to the court
D. All of the above

37. What is the required bond amount for a notary public and what type of bond is accepted?

A. $1,500 and cash deposit
B. $15,000 and bond from a surety insurer
C. $10,000 and personal check
D. $20,000 and bond from a bank

C. Record the revocation and its date on the notary public's certificate
D. Issues a new commission to the notary public

38. Which one of the following is not a reason for denial, revocation, or suspension of appointment and commission as a notary public by the Secretary of State?

A. Charging $20 to certify a photocopy of a power of attorney
B. Filing a police report for theft of a notary journal that was later found to be simply misplaced
C. Not paying child support for more than one year in California
D. Leaving a notary journal and seal unsecured on a desktop

39. To whom must a notary public surrender his journal to when there is reasonable evidence that the journal contains criminal evidence?

A. The notary public's employer
B. Secretary of State
C. A peace officer with probable cause
D. An auditor

40. What is the responsibility of the county clerk when the Secretary of State revokes a notary public's commission?

A. Nothing
B. Returns the commission to the notary public

PRACTICE TEST 1: ANSWER KEY

1. B. The Secretary of State can suspend the commission held by the notary public
2. C. Is acting as the agent for a beneficiary
3. C. A physical appearance before the notary public is required for acknowledgments or jurats
4. A. A jurat
5. C. Their official seal, if one is used for their office
6. B. 30 days
7. C. Investigating/pursuing commissioning and monetary remedies for violations of the notary public laws
8. A. Federal civil service employees currently working at the military reserve where they will be appointed
9. A. Charged with a felony
10. B. Not counted, with the last day counted unless it's Christmas Day
11. C. 18 years old
12. C. Both of the above
13. D. None of the above
14. B. Retained as proof and considered a valid record of the canceled check if the information on the front and back of the check is also electronically

29. A. The identity of the person who signed the document
30. A. Prescribed notice in English and the other language
31. B. A misdemeanor
Section 8209 (a)– Resignation, disqualification or removal of notary; records delivered to clerk; misdemeanor; death; destruction of records
32. A. A notary public may charge less than the maximum fee prescribed by law
33. C. None
34. D. A jurat
Section 8202 (b) – Execution of jurat; administration of oath or affirmation to affiant; attachment to affidavit
35. A. Only when the notary public is employed by a financial institution
36. B. Require the notary public to hand over their official seal to the court so the court can forward it to the Secretary of State
37. B. $15,000 and bond from a surety insurer
38. B. Filing a police report for theft of a notary journal that was later found to be simply misplaced
39. C. A peace officer with probable cause
Section 8206 (d) – Sequential journal; contents; thumbprint; loss of journal; copies of pages; exclusive property of notary public; limitations on surrender
40. C. Record the revocation and its date on the notary public's certificate

PRACTICE TEST 2: ANSWER SHEET

1. Ⓐ Ⓑ Ⓒ Ⓓ   11. Ⓐ Ⓑ Ⓒ Ⓓ   21. Ⓐ Ⓑ Ⓒ Ⓓ   31. Ⓐ Ⓑ Ⓒ Ⓓ

2. Ⓐ Ⓑ Ⓒ Ⓓ   12. Ⓐ Ⓑ Ⓒ Ⓓ   22. Ⓐ Ⓑ Ⓒ Ⓓ   32. Ⓐ Ⓑ Ⓒ Ⓓ

3. Ⓐ Ⓑ Ⓒ Ⓓ   13. Ⓐ Ⓑ Ⓒ Ⓓ   23. Ⓐ Ⓑ Ⓒ Ⓓ   33. Ⓐ Ⓑ Ⓒ Ⓓ

4. Ⓐ Ⓑ Ⓒ Ⓓ   14. Ⓐ Ⓑ Ⓒ Ⓓ   24. Ⓐ Ⓑ Ⓒ Ⓓ   34. Ⓐ Ⓑ Ⓒ Ⓓ

5. Ⓐ Ⓑ Ⓒ Ⓓ   15. Ⓐ Ⓑ Ⓒ Ⓓ   25. Ⓐ Ⓑ Ⓒ Ⓓ   35. Ⓐ Ⓑ Ⓒ Ⓓ

6. Ⓐ Ⓑ Ⓒ Ⓓ   16. Ⓐ Ⓑ Ⓒ Ⓓ   26. Ⓐ Ⓑ Ⓒ Ⓓ   36. Ⓐ Ⓑ Ⓒ Ⓓ

7. Ⓐ Ⓑ Ⓒ Ⓓ   17. Ⓐ Ⓑ Ⓒ Ⓓ   27. Ⓐ Ⓑ Ⓒ Ⓓ   37. Ⓐ Ⓑ Ⓒ Ⓓ

8. Ⓐ Ⓑ Ⓒ Ⓓ   18. Ⓐ Ⓑ Ⓒ Ⓓ   28. Ⓐ Ⓑ Ⓒ Ⓓ   38. Ⓐ Ⓑ Ⓒ Ⓓ

9. Ⓐ Ⓑ Ⓒ Ⓓ   19. Ⓐ Ⓑ Ⓒ Ⓓ   29. Ⓐ Ⓑ Ⓒ Ⓓ   39. Ⓐ Ⓑ Ⓒ Ⓓ

10. Ⓐ Ⓑ Ⓒ Ⓓ   20. Ⓐ Ⓑ Ⓒ Ⓓ   30. Ⓐ Ⓑ Ⓒ Ⓓ   40. Ⓐ Ⓑ Ⓒ Ⓓ

PRACTICE TEST 2 QUESTIONS

1. What is the consequence of violating the regulations adopted by the Secretary of State for approved vendors who provide notary public education?

   A. A civil penalty not exceeding $1,000 for each violation
   B. A civil penalty not exceeding $2,000 for each violation
   C. A civil penalty not exceeding $500
   D. No penalty or consequence

2. A notary public may do the following:

   A. Throw away the official seal when their commission expires so it can no longer be used
   B. Affix their self-inking stamp to every document the notary public signs, no exceptions
   C. Store their official seal in a locked drawer which no one may access except the notary public or their employer
   D. Use an embosser type of seal and a self-inking seal on the same document

3. When a surety of a notary public wishes to be released from responsibility for that notary public, the surety must:

   A. Offer the notary public a replacement surety bond written for higher risk insureds
   B. Apply to the superior court of the county where the notary public's oath and bond are filed

   C. Apply to the superior court of the county where the notary public's principal place of business is located
   D. Both B and C

4. Before an instrument can be recorded, its execution must be:

   A. Clear and legible
   B. Made in black ink only
   C. Acknowledged by the signer
   D. Acknowledged by the notary public

5. If a notary public surrenders his journal to a peace officer, how many days does the notary public have to notify the Secretary of State?

   A. 1 day
   B. 10 days
   C. 15 days
   D. 30 days

6. When can a notary public use the words notario publico?

   A. Only in certain counties
   B. Never because it is prohibited
   C. Only in the State of California
   D. Only if the notary public speaks fluent Spanish

7. What is the maximum statutory fee a notary public may charge for administering an oath or affirmation to one person and executing the jurat?

   A. $7

B. $30

C. $15

D. $0

8. Which of the following documents is required to be presented to a notary public as a condition for executing a jurat if the statement contains the affiant's birthdate or age, and includes a photograph or fingerprint of the person?

   A. A certified copy of the person's passport

   B. A certified copy of the person's marriage certificate

   C. A certified copy of the person's birth certificate

   D. An employment identification card

9. Which one of the following is considered a California state holiday for purposes of time computation?

   A. Boxing Day

   B. Rosa Parks Day

   C. Columbus Day

   D. Cesar Chavez Day

10. What is the responsibility of the Secretary of State with regard to notary seals?

    A. The Secretary of State is responsible for developing and implementing procedures and guidelines for the issuance of notary seals

    B. The Secretary of State is responsible for creating notary seals for all notaries

    C. The Secretary of State is responsible for selling notary seals to manufacturers and vendors

    D. The Secretary of State is responsible for establishing fees for notary seals

11. When the Secretary of State appoints and commissions state, city, county, and public school district employees as notaries public to act for and on behalf of the employing government entity, the notary public must:

    A. Relinquish their notary public journal and official seal to the employing government entity upon demand

    B. Remit all fees collected for notarial acts to the employing government entity

    C. Refuse to notarize any instrument that does not pertain to the employing government entity

    D. Pay the expense of their bond and notarial supplies

12. Dan is a notary public, and he is presented with a grant document that is missing the signature of the grantee. What should Dan do?

    A. Sign the grant document in his own handwriting and give a certificate of acknowledgment

    B. Refuse to accept any acknowledgment or proof of the incomplete instrument

    C. Ask the grantor to sign the grant document in his presence, then sign the certificate of acknowledgment

D. Ask the grantor to sign the grant document in his presence, then sign the grantee's signature and the certificate of acknowledgment

13. Which of the following must a notary public NOT be when notarizing a document that the notary public has a direct financial benefit to?

    A. Trustor or Trustee
    B. Employer
    C. Lawyer
    D. Agent

14. A person who is NOT a notary public but represents himself or herself as a notary public is guilty of a:

    A. Perjury
    B. Misdemeanor
    C. Felony
    D. Infraction

15. When a notary public submits an application for name change to the Secretary of State, the notary public's commission:

    A. Leaves all information unchanged for the rest of the commission term
    B. Reflects only the name change and leaves the commission number and commission term unchanged
    C. Reflects the name change, a new commission number, and restarts the term of the commission
    D. None of the above

16. What is required for a notary public to begin their term?

    A. File an official bond and an oath of office
    B. Submit an application to the Secretary of State
    C. Pay a fee to the county clerk
    D. Provide proof of insurance

17. A notary public may keep one notary journal for personal notarial acts and a second notary journal for notarial services related to their employment only if:

    A. Each journal is sequentially numbered
    B. Each journal is secured at all times in a locked area accessible to the notary public only
    C. Never
    D. Each journal is accompanied by its own official seal

18. The Secretary of State's disciplinary guidelines do which of the following:

    A. Facilitate due process
    B. Assist attorneys
    C. Maintain consistency
    D. All of the above

19. Rebecca falsely informs a notary that her husband has passed away and gives the notary a newly completed Grant Deed, which transfers the property into her name. She provides a falsified Affidavit of Death of Joint Tenancy to the notary stating that her husband had passed away. The notary notarizes the new Grant Deed and is unaware of the deception. If caught, Rebecca may face

which type of prosecution according to notary law?

A. A misdemeanor punishable by up to 1 year in prison
B. A felony punishable by up to 1 year in prison
C. A felony with a possible fine of up to $75,000
D. A felony punishable by up to 1 year in prison and a possible fine of up to $75,000

20. A notary public who is properly qualified and bonded as an immigration consultant may do which of the following?

A. Advertise their notarial services as long as the prescribed signage is displayed in both English and the alternate language
B. Complete immigration forms for a client with information provided by the client
C. Charge $20 for the service of completing immigration forms on behalf of a client
D. All of the above

21. A notary public may not receive any fee to notarize a military veteran's application for veteran's benefits unless:

A. The veteran or applicable signer voluntarily donates it to the notary public
B. The application or official document being signed is a request for

certified copies of a veteran's pension paperwork
C. The notary public is performing the notarization on a military base or reservation located anywhere in the state of California
D. A notary public may never receive compensation to notarize anything relating, directly or indirectly, to a veteran's pension

22. A notary public must refuse to notarize a document if:

A. It is handwritten
B. It is incomplete
C. It is on anything except white paper
D. None of the above

23. What type of criminal background information must be included on the application for notary public?

A. Felony convictions
B. A certain type of misdemeanor convictions
C. A simple jaywalking arrest awaiting appearance before the judge
D. All of the above

24. If a person manufactures an unauthorized replica of a notary public official seal with the intent to use same in a fraudulent act, he or she is guilty of:

A. Counterfeiting
B. Criminal impersonation
C. Copyright infringement
D. Forgery

25. Which form is most frequently completed by a notary public?

   A. A jurat
   B. A certificate of acknowledgment
   C. A certificate of title
   D. A certificate of signature by mark

26. Who can appoint a notary public to act on behalf of a governmental entity?

   A. Only the Governor of the state
   B. Only the employing governmental entity
   C. Only the Secretary of State
   D. Only a duly authorized representative of the governmental entity

27. If a notary public changes their business address to a new county, the notary public:

   A. May file a new oath and bond in the new county
   B. Must file a new oath and bond in the new county
   C. Can no longer perform notary services
   D. Must file a new oath and bond in the original county

28. What should two witnesses do when witnessing a signer's mark?

   A. Take a photo of the person
   B. Subscribe their own names as witnesses on the document
   C. Sign the document for the person
   D. Have the document notarized

29. How many notaries public may the Secretary of State appoint and commission in any given time period?

   A. No more than 100 per year
   B. No more than 500 per fiscal year
   C. As many as the Secretary of State thinks is enough
   D. No less than 100 but no more than 500 per calendar year

30. Proof of a signer's execution of an instrument, when not acknowledged, may be made by which one of the following?

   A. By a thumbprint of the signer affixed to the notary journal entry
   B. By the person who is actually signing the quit claim deed
   C. By the notary public
   D. By a subscribing witness

31. Which is the true statement?

   A. It is the notary's duty to draft power of attorney, mortgages and deeds when requested
   B. A notary does not have to charge a fee
   C. A notary may certify copies of marriage records
   D. A notary may give advice in relation to the legal document that is being notarized

32. A notary public who knowingly performs a fraudulent notarial act on a forged deed of trust for a single-family home containing no more than four dwelling units is guilty of:

A. An aggravated misdemeanor
B. Violation of the real estate
   administrative code
C. A felony
D. None of the above

33. Who must inform the Secretary of
    State when a notary public appointed
    and commissioned to a military
    reservation stops working at that
    military reserve?

    A. The notary public
    B. The U.S. Department of Defense
    C. The commanding officer of the
       military reserve
    D. The county clerk where the military
       reserve is located

34. An identification document needs the
    holder's:

    A. Photograph
    B. Signature
    C. Physical Description
    D. All of the above

35. A protest is a certificate of dishonor
    made by a:

    A. Clerk of the United States
       Department of the Treasury
    B. Notary public employed by an
       insurance agency
    C. Notary public employed by a
       financial institution
    D. None of the above

36. A notary public who fails to obtain
    satisfactory evidence as to a signer's

true and accurate identity is subject to a
_____ penalty not exceeding $____:

A. Criminal; not less than $10,000
B. Civil; not more than $2,500
C. Criminal; not more than $2,500
D. Civil; not more than $10,000

37. What happens to a notary public's
    commission and seal upon conviction
    of an offense?

    A. Commission and seal will not be
       affected
    B. Commission is suspended, seal must
       be destroyed
    C. Commission is revoked, seal given
       to the county clerk
    D. Commission is revoked, seal
       surrendered to the court

38. A peace officer acting within proper
    authority may request, receive, and
    examine which of the following items
    relating to the official acts of a notary
    public?

    A. Notary journal
    B. E-mails and/or text messages on
       the notary public's phone
    C. The notary public's application,
       background check, and commission
       paperwork
    D. All of the above

39. Who can assist a client in completing
    immigration forms?

    A. Any notary public
    B. Only an attorney

C. Only a U.S. Department of Justice representative

D. A registered California Secretary of State immigration consultant

40. The Secretary of State shall assign what to each notary public with their commission?

A. A certificate of commission

B. A sequential identification number

C. A commission expiration date

D. None of the above

PRACTICE TEST 2: ANSWER KEY

1. A. A civil penalty not exceeding $1,000 for each violation

Section 8201.2 (d)(1) – Review of course of study for notary public; approval of education course of study, violation of regulations; civil penalties .... Page 52

2. D. Use an embosser type of seal and a self-inking seal on the same document

Notary Public Seal.. Page 8

3. C. Apply to the superior court of the county where the notary public's principal place of business is located

Section 8216 – Release of surety .... Page 86

4. C. Acknowledged by the signer

Section 27287 – Acknowledgment of execution or proof by subscribing witness required before recording; exceptions .... Page 103

5. B. 10 days

Section 8206 (d) – Sequential journal; contents; thumbprint; loss of journal; copies of pages; exclusive property of notary public; limitations on surrender .... Page 64

6. B. Never because it is prohibited

Section 8219.5 (c) – Advertising in language other than English; posting of notice relating to legal advice and fees; translation of notary public into Spanish; suspension .... Page 87

7. C. $15

Section 8211 – Fees .... Page 73

8. C. A certified copy of the person's birth certificate

Section 8230 (a) – Identification of affiant; verification .... Page 96

9. D. Cesar Chavez Day

Section 12 (a) – Computation of time; holidays; application of section .... Page 120

10. A. The Secretary of State is responsible for developing and implementing procedures and guidelines for the issuance of notary seals

Section 8207.2 (b) – Manufacture, duplication, and sale of seal or stamp; procedures and guidelines for issuance of seals; certificate of authorization.. Page 68

11. B. Remit all fees collected for notarial acts to the employing government entity

Section 8202.5 – State, county and school employees; certificates; expenses .... Page 55

12. B. Refuse to accept any acknowledgment or proof of the incomplete instrument

Section 8205 (2) – Duties... Page 61

13. A. Trustor or Trustee

Section 8224 (b) – Conflict of interest; financial or beneficial interest in transaction;

28. B. Subscribe their own names as witnesses on the document

Signature by Mark .... Page 28

29. C. As many as the Secretary of State thinks is enough

Section 8200 – Appointment and commission; number; jurisdiction .... Page 49

30. D. By a subscribing witness

Section 1195 (a)(2) – Proof of execution; methods; certificate form .... Page 113

31. B. A notary does not have to charge a fee

Fees .... Page 39

32. C. A felony

Section 8214.2 (a) – Fraud relating to deed of trust; single-family residence .... Page 82

33. C. The commanding officer of the military reserve

Section 8203.4 – Military and naval reservations; term of office; termination .... Page 59

34. D. All of the above

Section 1185 (1)(A) – Acknowledgments; requisites .... Page 106

35. C. Notary public employed by a financial institution

Section 3505 (b) – Protest, Noting for protest .... Page 126

36. D. Civil; not more than $10,000

Section 1185 (b)(1)(B) – Acknowledgments; requisites .... Page 106

37. D. Commission is revoked, seal surrendered to the court

Section 8214.8 – Revocation upon certain convictions .... Page 86

38. D. All of the above

Section 8228 – Enforcement of a chapter; examination of notarial books .... Page 95

39. D. A registered California Secretary of State immigration consultant

Immigration Documents .... Page 35

40. B. A sequential identification number

Section 8207.1 – Identification Number .... Page 68

PRACTICE TEST 3: ANSWER SHEET

1. Ⓐ Ⓑ Ⓒ Ⓓ   11. Ⓐ Ⓑ Ⓒ Ⓓ   21. Ⓐ Ⓑ Ⓒ Ⓓ   31. Ⓐ Ⓑ Ⓒ Ⓓ

2. Ⓐ Ⓑ Ⓒ Ⓓ   12. Ⓐ Ⓑ Ⓒ Ⓓ   22. Ⓐ Ⓑ Ⓒ Ⓓ   32. Ⓐ Ⓑ Ⓒ Ⓓ

3. Ⓐ Ⓑ Ⓒ Ⓓ   13. Ⓐ Ⓑ Ⓒ Ⓓ   23. Ⓐ Ⓑ Ⓒ Ⓓ   33. Ⓐ Ⓑ Ⓒ Ⓓ

4. Ⓐ Ⓑ Ⓒ Ⓓ   14. Ⓐ Ⓑ Ⓒ Ⓓ   24. Ⓐ Ⓑ Ⓒ Ⓓ   34. Ⓐ Ⓑ Ⓒ Ⓓ

5. Ⓐ Ⓑ Ⓒ Ⓓ   15. Ⓐ Ⓑ Ⓒ Ⓓ   25. Ⓐ Ⓑ Ⓒ Ⓓ   35. Ⓐ Ⓑ Ⓒ Ⓓ

6. Ⓐ Ⓑ Ⓒ Ⓓ   16. Ⓐ Ⓑ Ⓒ Ⓓ   26. Ⓐ Ⓑ Ⓒ Ⓓ   36. Ⓐ Ⓑ Ⓒ Ⓓ

7. Ⓐ Ⓑ Ⓒ Ⓓ   17. Ⓐ Ⓑ Ⓒ Ⓓ   27. Ⓐ Ⓑ Ⓒ Ⓓ   37. Ⓐ Ⓑ Ⓒ Ⓓ

8. Ⓐ Ⓑ Ⓒ Ⓓ   18. Ⓐ Ⓑ Ⓒ Ⓓ   28. Ⓐ Ⓑ Ⓒ Ⓓ   38. Ⓐ Ⓑ Ⓒ Ⓓ

9. Ⓐ Ⓑ Ⓒ Ⓓ   19. Ⓐ Ⓑ Ⓒ Ⓓ   29. Ⓐ Ⓑ Ⓒ Ⓓ   39. Ⓐ Ⓑ Ⓒ Ⓓ

10. Ⓐ Ⓑ Ⓒ Ⓓ   20. Ⓐ Ⓑ Ⓒ Ⓓ   30. Ⓐ Ⓑ Ⓒ Ⓓ   40. Ⓐ Ⓑ Ⓒ Ⓓ

PRACTICE TEST 3 QUESTIONS

1. What is an employing government entity required to do with any fees remitted by a notary public employee?

   A. Forward said funds to the Secretary of State
   B. Deposit the fees into a state fund for notary public education
   C. Save the fees to a petty cash fund for employee luncheons
   D. Deposit the fees into the payroll account that funds the notary public's wages

2. Which of the following may be a document of "satisfactory evidence"?

   A. An expired Oregon driver's license that was issued in 2017
   B. An ID card issued by a Californian church
   C. An employee ID card issued by the California Department of Justice
   D. A certified copy of the signer's birth certificate

3. Which of the following is true regarding a person's right to a hearing after a denial of an application for a notary public commission?

   A. He or she shall have a right to a hearing
   B. He or she shall have a right to a hearing if the Secretary of State has not previously denied or revoked their application or commission
   C. He or she shall have a right to a hearing if the Secretary of State has found that the applicant has constituted grounds for suspension of a notary public's commission
   D. He or she shall not have a right to a hearing if the Secretary of State has previously denied or revoked their application or commission within one year

4. Which of the following is true regarding notary public and immigration matters?

   A. A notary public cannot advertise as an immigration specialist
   B. A notary public can provide immigration services without proper certification
   C. Notary publics can only enter data on immigration forms at the direction of a client
   D. Notary publics cannot enter data on immigration forms provided by a federal or state agency

5. A certified copy of a veteran's pension application may be provided only to:

   A. No one except the veteran, in person
   B. Any state, county, or city agency that requests it
   C. Any United States official who provides the request in writing
   D. None of the above

6. If a completed notarial act is found to be incorrect, what should the notary public do first?

A. Destroy the document with the incorrect notarization and request a new one
B. Strike out the incorrect part and write in the accurate information
C. Notarize the document all over again
D. Contact the Secretary of State

7. If a notary public is notarizing a deed of trust, what additional information must be recorded in the notary journal?

A. The signer's date of birth
B. The signer's thumbprint
C. Address or legal description of real property named in the deed of trust
D. The signer's occupation and work address (if applicable)

8. What is a vendor required to have before they can manufacture and sell a notary seal or embosser stamp?

A. Approval from the State Department of Justice
B. Approval from the State Department of Consumer Affairs
C. Approval from the State Department of General Services
D. None of the above

9. What is true about death certificates?

A. They must be notarized to be officially recognized
B. They cannot be notarized
C. They are filed with the IRS
D. They are filed with the county clerk

10. If a notary public refuses to relinquish

their notary journal to a peace officer upon request is subject to a civil penalty of:

A. No less than $2,500
B. No less than $1,500
C. No more than $2,500
D. No more than $1,000

11. The prescribed boxed notice on a certificate for proof of execution must be located:

A. Anywhere within the proof of execution
B. At the top of the proof of execution
C. At the bottom of the proof of execution
D. Directly below the notary public's signature on the proof of execution

12. The written examination prescribed by the California Secretary of State for notary public applicants is:

A. Six hours long
B. Three hours long
C. Based upon the contents of the California Secretary of State's Notary Public Handbook
D. Based upon the federal laws governing United States notaries public

13. Forgery of a notary public seal or signature is punishable by:

A. Imprisonment for less than one year in county jail
B. Imprisonment for 2 years, 3 years, or 4 years in prison

C. Financial restitution only to the injured party in an amount equal to the damages suffered by the injured party

D. Imprisonment in a federal facility for no less than 2 years

14. A subscribing witness is not:

A. Less than 21 years of age
B. Allowed to accept a verbal acknowledgment of prior signing
C. Allowed to subscribe an instrument unless specifically requested to do so by the signer
D. Allowed to work for a notary public

15. How long can a notary public be prosecuted for giving their official seal to an unauthorized person?

A. Within four years after the violation was finished
B. Within four years after the violation was discovered
C. Both A & B, whichever is sooner
D. Both A & B, whichever is later

16. What is one type of satisfactory evidence?

A. Identifying documents
B. Personal knowledge
C. Signature by mark
D. Proof or acknowledgment

17. What are the qualifications for a notary public applicant to take a three-hour notary public education class?

A. If the notary public applicant has not changed their place of business since the last application
B. If the notary public applicant has an unexpired commission
C. If the notary public applicant is currently commissioned or their commission has only been expired less than 30 days
D. If the applicant is 21 or older

18. What information shall accompany the name of the state in a jurat signed on a military reservation?

A. The date the instrument was signed
B. The name of the military reservation
C. The expiration date of the notary public's commission
D. All of the above

19. What documents require the party signing the document to place their right thumbprint in the notary's journal?

A. Deed, quitclaim deed, deed of trust, or other document affecting real property, or a power of attorney document
B. All acknowledgments, but not jurats
C. Any notarization regardless of the nature of the document
D. All document signers, credible witnesses and/or subscribing witnesses

20. When a signer is taking an oath, the signer:

A. Must raise right hand
B. Must raise left hand
C. Must repeat oath

D. May raise right hand but this is not required

21. Max is filling out an application for a notary public commission. He was arrested for a DUI six months ago, but his trial has not yet taken place. What should Max do?

   A. Disclose the arrest for the DUI on the application because the trial is still pending
   B. Wait until the trial is over to disclose the arrest on the application
   C. Not disclose the arrest on the application because it has not yet resulted in a conviction
   D. Contact the Secretary of State's office to ask if he should disclose the arrest on the application

22. A certificate of acknowledgment is a notary public's certification of:

   A. The age of the person signing the document
   B. The person's location at the time of signing the document
   C. Both of the above
   D. None of the above

23. What is the fine for overcharging the fee for a notarial service?

   A. Up to $75
   B. Up to $750
   C. Up to $1,000
   D. Up to $1,500

24. What can a notary public do regarding charges for immigration forms?

   A. Charge $20 per set of forms
   B. Cannot charge for immigration forms at all
   C. Charge up to $15 per set of forms
   D. Charge up to $15 per set of forms only if the notary is an attorney

25. What is the exception that would require the two witnesses who witnessed the signing by mark to sign the notary public's journal?

   A. If the witnesses were acting in the capacity of credible witnesses in establishing the identity of the person signing by mark
   B. If the witnesses were not present at the time of signing
   C. If the witnesses were family members of the signer
   D. If the witnesses refused to sign the document

26. Any non-attorney notary public who advertises their notarial services with signs posted in a language other than English must do which of the following:

   A. Employ an interpreter who shall be present on the premises during business hours
   B. Prominently post a sign in both English and the other language which says "I am not an attorney but I can answer any legal questions you may have"
   C. Prominently post a sign which lists the statutory maximum fee a notary public may charge for various notarial services

D. All of the above

27. Which of the following statements is true regarding manufacturers or vendors authorized to issue notary seals?

    A. They can issue notary seals without obtaining a permit from the Secretary of State

    B. They must obtain a permit from the Secretary of State before issuing notary seals

    C. They must pay a fee to the Secretary of State to become authorized to issue notary seals

    D. The fee charged by the Secretary of State for the issuance of the permit is $100

28. A Camp Pendleton notary public may charge which fee for certifying a copy of a power of attorney?

    A. $5
    B. $15
    C. $0
    D. $25

29. Signers of the following documents must leave a right thumbprint:

    A. Articles of incorporation
    B. Documents affecting real property
    C. Powers of attorney
    D. B & C

30. Maria is a state employee who is also a notary public that was appointed to act for and on behalf of the state. Who can pay for Maria's bond premiums and cost of stamps and other supplies?

    A. Only the state of California
    B. Only a city in California
    C. Only a school district in California
    D. The state of California or any city, county, or school district in California

31. A certification of a copy of a power of attorney must state the certifying person has:

    A. Examined the copy of the power of the attorney, verified the identity of the signer, belief the copy is true, and belief the copy is accurate

    B. Examined the original power of attorney, examined the copy of the power of attorney, belief the copy is true, and belief the copy is accurate

    C. Examined the copy of the power of attorney, verified the identity of the signer, belief the copy is true, and the copy is believed to be accurate

    D. Examined the original power of attorney, examined the signatures of the principal and the attorney-in-fact, agreed the copy to be complete, and agreed the copy is properly dated

32. Where can a notary public perform their services?

    A. In any part of California
    B. Only in certain parts of California
    C. Only in specific counties of California
    D. In any part of the United States

33. A notary public who is not properly qualified and bonded as an immigration specialist may only enter data on

immigration forms with information provided by a client if:

A. The client is a personal friend and the notary public is not completing the forms in a professional capacity
B. The notary public has a waiver from the Secretary of State
C. The notary public doubles the amount of their bond on file
D. None of the above

34. The _____ and form of maps is governed by the provisions of article §66433. Fill in the blank.

A. Materials
B. Color
C. Size
D. Content

35. Eric, a notary public, was asked to take an affidavit from Jane for submission before the court. What is Eric's duty as a notary public in this scenario?

A. Eric is not required to take Jane's affidavit as it is not an incident to the duties of his office
B. Eric must take Jane's affidavit, but he can delegate the task of signing it to a witness
C. Eric must take Jane's affidavit and sign it himself in his own handwriting
D. Eric must take Jane's affidavit, but he can ask Jane to sign it herself

36. What is the maximum statutory fee a notary public may charge to notarize a signature on a vote by mail ballot identification envelope?

A. $7
B. $30
C. $15
D. $0

37. Which of the following is signed in the presence of the notary?

A. Acknowledgment
B. Jurat
C. Certificate
D. None of the above

38. If a notary public commits misconduct or neglect in their duties the notary public is:

A. Able to be personally sued in a civil action by all person(s) injured by the misconduct or neglect
B. Not able to be personally sued in a civil action by all person(s) injured by the misconduct or neglect
C. Protected by their surety bond, like an insurance policy
D. None of the above

39. Where can a notary public take and subscribe the oath of office?

A. In any county clerk's office
B. In the office of the Secretary of State
C. In the office of any notary public of the state
D. In the office of that county clerk or before another notary public in that county

40. Which of the following is a valid form of identification a notary public may

accept to certify a signer's identity?

A. An expired U.S. passport that was issued in 2020

B. A library card

C. A supermarket discount card with the signer's name and address

D. A current credit card issued by any financial institution doing business in the state of California as long as it bears the signer's full name and signature

PRACTICE TEST 3: ANSWER KEY

1. D. Deposit the fees into the payroll account that funds the notary public's wages
Section 8202.5 – State, county and school district employees; certificates .... Page 55

2. C. An employee ID card issued by the California Department of Justice
Section 1185 (b)(4)(E) – Acknowledgments; requisites .... Page 106

3. D. He or she shall not have a right to a hearing if the Secretary of State has previously denied or revoked their application or commission within one year
Section 8214.3 (b) – Hearing prior to denial or revocation of commission or imposition of civil penalties; law governing; exceptions .... Page 84

4. A. A notary public cannot advertise as an immigration specialist
Immigration Documents .... Page 35

5. C. Any United States official who provides the request in writing
Section 6107 (b)(4) – Veterans .... Page 99

6. C. Notarize the document all over again
Correcting a Notarial Act .... Page 33

7. B. The signer's thumbprint
Section 8206 (a)(1)(2) – Sequential journal; contents; thumbprint; loss of journal; copies of pages; exclusive property of notary public; limitations on surrender .... Page 63

8. D. None of the above
Section 8207.2 – Manufacture, duplication, and sale of seal or stamp; procedures and guidelines for issuance of seals; certificate of authorization .... Page 68

9. B. Cannot be notarized
Certified Copies .... Page 33

10. C. No more than $2,500
Section 8214.21 – Failure to provide access to the sequential journal of notarial acts; civil penalties .... Page 82

11. B. At the top of the proof of execution
Section 1195 (b)(c) – Proof of execution; methods; certificate form .... Page 114

12. C. Based upon the contents of the California Secretary of State's Notary Public Handbook
Section 8201 – Qualifications to be a notary public; proof of course completion; reappointment .... Page 49

13. A. Imprisonment for less than one year in county jail
Section 473 – Forgery; punishment .... Page 132

14. C. Allowed to subscribe an instrument unless specifically requested to do so by the signer

Section 1935 – Subscribing witness defined .... Page 120

15. D. Both A & B, whichever is later

Section 8228.1 (b) – Willful failure to perform duty or control notarial seal .... Page 95

16. A. Identifying documents

Identification .... Page 10

17. B. If the notary public applicant has an unexpired commission

Notary Public Education .... Page 3

18. D. All of the above

Section 8203.5 – Military and naval reservations, jurat .... Page 60

19. A. Deed, quitclaim deed, deed of trust, or other document affecting real property, or a power of attorney document

Section 8206 (G) – Sequential journal; contents; thumbprint; loss of journal; copies of pages; exclusive property of notary public; limitations on surrender .... Page 63

20. D. May raise right hand but this is not required

Jurat .... Page 21

21. A. Disclose the arrest for the DUI on the application because the trial is still pending

Convictions .... Page 2

22. B. The person's location at the time of signing the document

Acknowledgment .... Page 18

23. B. Up to $750

Section 8214.15 (b) – Civil penalties .... Page 81

24. C. Charge up to $15 per set of forms

Immigration Documents .... Page 35

25. A. If the witnesses were acting in the capacity of credible witnesses in establishing the identity of the person signing by mark

Signature by Mark .... Page 28

26. C. Prominently post a sign which lists the statutory maximum fee a notary public may charge for various notarial services

Section 8219.5 (a)(2) – Advertising in a language other than English; posting of notice relating to legal advice and fees; translation of notary public into Spanish .... Page 87

27. B. They must obtain a permit from the Secretary of State before issuing notary seals

Section 8207.2 (c) – Manufacture, duplication, and sale of seal or stamp; procedures and guidelines for issuance of seals; certificate of authorization .... Page 68

28. C. $0

PRACTICE TEST 4: ANSWER SHEET

1. Ⓐ Ⓑ Ⓒ Ⓓ   11. Ⓐ Ⓑ Ⓒ Ⓓ   21. Ⓐ Ⓑ Ⓒ Ⓓ   31. Ⓐ Ⓑ Ⓒ Ⓓ

2. Ⓐ Ⓑ Ⓒ Ⓓ   12. Ⓐ Ⓑ Ⓒ Ⓓ   22. Ⓐ Ⓑ Ⓒ Ⓓ   32. Ⓐ Ⓑ Ⓒ Ⓓ

3. Ⓐ Ⓑ Ⓒ Ⓓ   13. Ⓐ Ⓑ Ⓒ Ⓓ   23. Ⓐ Ⓑ Ⓒ Ⓓ   33. Ⓐ Ⓑ Ⓒ Ⓓ

4. Ⓐ Ⓑ Ⓒ Ⓓ   14. Ⓐ Ⓑ Ⓒ Ⓓ   24. Ⓐ Ⓑ Ⓒ Ⓓ   34. Ⓐ Ⓑ Ⓒ Ⓓ

5. Ⓐ Ⓑ Ⓒ Ⓓ   15. Ⓐ Ⓑ Ⓒ Ⓓ   25. Ⓐ Ⓑ Ⓒ Ⓓ   35. Ⓐ Ⓑ Ⓒ Ⓓ

6. Ⓐ Ⓑ Ⓒ Ⓓ   16. Ⓐ Ⓑ Ⓒ Ⓓ   26. Ⓐ Ⓑ Ⓒ Ⓓ   36. Ⓐ Ⓑ Ⓒ Ⓓ

7. Ⓐ Ⓑ Ⓒ Ⓓ   17. Ⓐ Ⓑ Ⓒ Ⓓ   27. Ⓐ Ⓑ Ⓒ Ⓓ   37. Ⓐ Ⓑ Ⓒ Ⓓ

8. Ⓐ Ⓑ Ⓒ Ⓓ   18. Ⓐ Ⓑ Ⓒ Ⓓ   28. Ⓐ Ⓑ Ⓒ Ⓓ   38. Ⓐ Ⓑ Ⓒ Ⓓ

9. Ⓐ Ⓑ Ⓒ Ⓓ   19. Ⓐ Ⓑ Ⓒ Ⓓ   29. Ⓐ Ⓑ Ⓒ Ⓓ   39. Ⓐ Ⓑ Ⓒ Ⓓ

10. Ⓐ Ⓑ Ⓒ Ⓓ   20. Ⓐ Ⓑ Ⓒ Ⓓ   30. Ⓐ Ⓑ Ⓒ Ⓓ   40. Ⓐ Ⓑ Ⓒ Ⓓ

PRACTICE TEST 4 QUESTIONS

1. What is the requirement for a notary public applying for reappointment?

   A. Completion of three-hour refresher course
   B. Completion of one-hour course
   C. Completion of six-hour course
   D. No requirement for any course

2. Which one of the following statements is true about a notary public changing their address?

   A. A notary public must provide their change of address information to the Secretary of State within 30 days
   B. A notary public is only required to report a change in primary business address to the Secretary of State
   C. When a business relocates to a different county a new oath of office and bond must be filed with the county clerk in the new county
   D. The written notice can be submitted in letter form or e-mail

3. A notary public presents a vendor with their certificate of authorization in order to obtain an official notary seal. What must the vendor with the certificate of authorization?

   A. Submit the original certificate of authorization to the Secretary of State only
   B. Submit both the original and a copy of the certificate of authorization to the Secretary of State

   C. Retain a copy of original certificate of authorization and submit the original to the Secretary of State
   D. Does not need to submit any certificate of authorization to the Secretary of State

4. A witness is proved to be a subscribing witness by:

   A. A note from the subscribing witness's mom
   B. A document which complies with the "satisfactory evidence" definition
   C. A waiver provided by the Secretary of State
   D. The oath of another credible witness who provides satisfactory evidence of their own identity and who personally knows both the subscribing witness and the notary public

5. Who can notarize a document executed by a notary public?

   A. A judge
   B. The county clerk
   C. The Secretary of State
   D. A different notary public

6. When notifying the Secretary of State that a journal has been surrendered, the notary must also include:

   A. A copy of the receipt for the journal

B. The commission number and expiration date of the notary

C. The period of journal entries

D. All of the above

7. John knowingly destroyed a notary public's records, causing harm to Mary. What is the penalty for John's actions?

A. John may be subject to a civil action for damages to Mary

B. John may only be charged with a misdemeanor

C. Prosecution for John's offense must be commenced within four years of the discovery of the offense

D. John may be subject to exclusive remedies for his offense

8. A person authorized to administer an oath or affirmation may be:

A. A notary public

B. A shorthand reporter

C. Both of the above

D. None of the above

9. Prior to granting an appointment as a notary public, the Secretary of State shall determine if the applicant possesses what four things to fulfill the responsibilities of the position?

A. A good credit score, positive character references, honesty, and truthfulness

B. Honesty, credibility, truthfulness, and integrity

C. Credibility, honesty, high school diploma or GED, and no criminal record

D. All of the above

10. A notary public is authorized to receive a fee for which of the following?

A. Notarizing a deed of trust for a military veteran

B. Certifying an oath of office

C. Any notarial act performed on a military base or reservation

D. Administering an oath

11. An officer designated by the Secretary of State to investigate and enforce all laws pertaining to notaries public is called a(n):

A. Administrative officer

B. Peace officer

C. Corrections officer

D. Court officer

12. What is the effect of a certified copy of a power of attorney that has been certified by a notary public?

A. It has the same force and effect as the original power of attorney

B. It has less force and effect than the original power of attorney

C. It has more force and effect than the original power of attorney

D. It has no force or effect

13. Which form contains the language "Subscribed and sworn to (or affirmed)"?

A. A certificate of acknowledgment

B. A signature by mark

C. A jurat

D. A certification of a copy of a Power of Attorney

14. If a notary public fails to obtain a thumbprint from a signer when necessary is subject to a civil penalty of:

   A. No more than $1,000
   B. No more than $1,500
   C. No more than $2,000
   D. None of the above

15. The oath of a single credible witness may only be used to identify the signer if:

   A. The single credible witness personally knows the signer
   B. The single credible witness personally knows the notary public
   C. The single credible witness has no financial interest in the document being signed
   D. All of the above

16. When a notary public takes an acknowledgment of an instrument, he/she must attach:

   A. Nothing, if he/she has signed the on instrument itself
   B. A certificate, if she hasn't signed the instrument itself
   C. Both of the above
   D. None of the above

17. What is the fee a notary public appointed on a military or naval reservation may charge to notarize a certificate of acknowledgment?

   A. $5
   B. $15
   C. $0
   D. The commanding officer of the military or naval reserve determines what fees the notary public may charge

18. Can a private employer pay for a notary public's bond, stamps, or supplies?

   A. No, it is illegal
   B. Yes, but only with a written agreement
   C. Yes, but only if the notary remits all fees to the employer
   D. Yes, but only if the employer is a government agency

19. A felony is a crime that is punishable with one or more of the following:

   A. Death
   B. Imprisonment in state prison
   C. Imprisonment in county jail
   D. All of the above

20. The following may be used to provide evidence of the execution of an instrument when it has not been acknowledged:

   A. A subscribing witness
   B. The party executing it
   C. Other witnesses
   D. All of the above

21. Where must a notary public file their oath and surety bond?

A. In the county of their residence
B. Anywhere within the state of California
C. In the county where their place of business is located
D. In every county where the notary public conducts business

22. A subscribing witness is a person who:

A. Sees a writing executed
B. Hears a proof of execution
C. Signs his name as a witness to an execution
D. All of the above

23. Certified copies of birth, fetal death, death, and marriage records are made by:

A. A Court Registrar
B. A County Registrar
C. A Municipal Registrar
D. A State Registrar

24. Every appointed notary public must execute an official bond in the amount of:

A. $25,000
B. $5,000
C. Amount varies by surety bond company
D. None of the above

25. When a notary public transfers counties and elects to make a new filing, what must the notary public do within 30 days?

A. Obtain an official seal

B. Obtain a new commission
C. Pay new fees
D. Both A and C

26. If a notary public fails to comply with the advertising and signage requirements in Section 8219.5 of the Government Code:

A. The first offense is punishable by the suspension of the notary public's commission for no less than one year or revocation of the notary public's commission
B. The second offense is punishable by permanent revocation of the notary public's commission
C. Both A and B
D. None of the above

27. A notary acknowledgment on certain maps may be deemed sufficient for recording without the notary public's official seal if the following items are typed or printed near the notary public's signature:

A. The notary public's residential address and phone number
B. The date the notary public was commissioned
C. The county where the acknowledgment is being made
D. The notary public's primary business address

28. A manufacturer or vendor may provide a notary public with an official seal only if:

A. The notary public is over 18 years of age
B. The notary public supplies the manufacturer/vendor with a certificate of authorization
C. The notary public provides photo identification
D. The notary public remits payment in advance

29. What is the requirement for a notary public to perform a marriage?

A. Be a judge or lawyer
B. Be a priest, minister, or rabbi
C. Have approval from the Secretary of State
D. Live in the county where the marriage takes place

30. The Secretary of State may refuse to appoint any applicant as a notary public or terminate/revoke/suspend the commission of any notary public for which of the following:

A. Charging $15 to administer an oath or affirmation to one person
B. Notarizing immigration documents
C. Advertising one's notarial status with the words "Notario" or "Notario Publico"
D. Having a GED instead of a high school diploma

31. A notary public may perform which of the following notarial acts?

A. Notarize their parent's signature on a Last Will and Testament which divides all property and debt equally

amongst the notary public and their siblings
B. Notarize the tenant's signature on a Rental Agreement for an apartment owned by the notary public's ex-spouse who is paying the notary public spousal maintenance from their divorce
C. Notarize their current spouse's signature on a
D. Notarize an agreement for a portion of the vending profits from a leased soda machine in their office.

32. What must a private employer do before paying for its notary public employee's bond and official seal?

A. Obtain a criminal background check on the employee
B. Enter into a specific agreement with the employee to pay expenses related to the employee's notary public commission
C. Report the employee's business address to the Secretary of State
D. Require the employee to sign a promissory note

33. What is the fine for failing to immediately notify the Secretary of State if you lost your official stamp or journal?

A. Up to $75
B. Up to $750
C. Up to $1,500
D. Up to $2,000

34. Notaries must:

A. Keep a photocopy of every instrument notarized
B. Keep their journal in a locked and secured area
C. Refuse service to a non-Californian resident
D. None of the above

35. A notary may not notarize:

A. When he/she is the attorney who drafted the papers
B. When he/she is a real estate agent who sold the property
C. For a spouse
D. When he/she is a mortgagor in a transaction

36. What information should be included in the notification sent to the Secretary of State if a notary public's sequential journal of official acts is lost or stolen, and when should it be sent?

A. The period of the journal entries, the notary public commission number, and the expiration date of the commission, and when applicable, a photocopy of any police report that specifies the theft; it should be sent immediately
B. Only the notary public commission number and the expiration date of the commission; it should be sent within 30 days of the loss or theft
C. Only a photocopy of any police report that specifies the theft of the sequential journal of official acts; it should be sent within 10 business days of the loss or theft

D. The name and address of the notary public, and the date of the loss or theft; it should be sent within 90 days of the loss or theft

37. When a check has not been honored for payment, the Secretary of State shall give a written notice. If no correction is done, a second notice of cancellation shall be given at least:

A. 10 days
B. 20 days
C. 30 days
D. 60 days

38. If a document that contains the age or birthdate of the signer has a jurat for the notary public to execute, the notary public must see:

A. Two forms of identification with at least one of them bearing a photograph
B. A certified copy of the signer's birth certificate
C. The oath of a credible witness as to the signer's age, plus the thumbprint of the signer
D. A valid driver's license or identification card

39. A written request to a notary public from any member of the public seeking information and/or copies of a notarial act must include:

A. Not applicable. Such requests must go through the Secretary of State, not through the notary public

B. The county in which the notarial act was performed

C. The type of document

D. The amount charged for the notarial act, if known

40. What is required to be included in a notary public sequential journal if identity was established based on the oaths or affirmation of two credible witnesses?

A. The signatures of the credible witnesses, type of identifying documents, identifying numbers of the documents, and the dates of issuance or expiration of the documents presented by the witnesses to establish their identities

B. The signatures of the person making the acknowledgment or taking the oath or affirmation

C. A statement that the identity of the person making the acknowledgment or taking the oath or affirmation was based on satisfactory evidence

D. None of the above

PRACTICE TEST 4: ANSWER KEY

1. A. Completion of three-hour refresher course

Section 8201 (b)(2) – Qualifications to be a notary public; proof of course completion; reappointment .... Page 49

2. A. A notary public must provide their change of address information to the Secretary of State within 30 days

Change of Address .... Page 41

3. C. Retain a copy of original certificate of authorization and submit the original to the Secretary of State

Section 8207.3 – Certificates of authorization; authorization to provide seal; lost, misplaced, damaged or otherwise unworkable seal .... Page 69

4. D. The oath of another credible witness who provides satisfactory evidence of their own identity and who personally knows both the subscribing witness and the notary public

Section 1196 – Subscribing witness; establishment of identity .... Page 116

5. D. A different notary public

Section 8224.1 – Writings, depositions, or affidavits of notary public; prohibitions against proof or taking by that notary public .... Page 92

6. D. All of the above

Section 8206 (G)(d) – Sequential journal; contents; thumbprint; loss of journal; copies of pages; exclusive property of notary public; limitations on surrender .... Page 63

7. A. John may be subject to a civil action for damages to Mary

Section 8221 – Destruction, defacement or concealment of records or papers; misdemeanor; liability for damages .... Page 89

8. C. Both of the above

Section 2093 (b) – Officers authorized to administer oaths or affirmations .... Page 121

9. B. Honesty, credibility, truthfulness, and integrity

Section 8201.1 (a) – Additional qualifications; determination; identification .... Page 50

10. A. Notarizing a deed of trust for a military veteran

Section 6108 – Oaths of office; claim against counties .... Page 100

11. B. Peace officer

Section 830.3 (o) – Peace officers; employing agencies; authority .... Page 131

12. A. It has the same force and effect as the original power of attorney

Powers of Attorney – Certifying .... Page 31

13. C. A jurat

misplaced, damaged or otherwise unworkable seal .... Page 69

29. B. Be a priest, minister, or rabbi
Confidential Marriage Licenses .... Page 36

30. C. Advertising one's notarial status with the words "Notario" or "Notario Publico"
Section 8214.1 (f) – Grounds for refusal, revocation of commission .... Page 79

31. B. Notarize the tenant's signature on a Rental Agreement for an apartment owned by the
notary public's ex-spouse who is paying the notary public spousal maintenance from their
divorce
Section 8224 (b) – Conflict of interest; financial interest in a transaction .... Page 92

32. B. Enter into a specific agreement with the employee to pay expenses related to the
employee's notary public commission
Section 8202.7 – Private employers; agreement to pay premium on bonds and costs of
supplies; remission of fees to employer .... Page 56

33. C. Up to $1,500
Section 8207.4 – Violations; penalties .... Page 70

34. B. Keep their journal in a locked and secured area
Notary Public Journal .... Page 14

35. D. When he/she is a mortgagor in a transaction
Section 8224 – Conflict of interest; financial interest in a transaction .... Page 92

36. A. The period of the journal entries, the notary public commission number, and the
expiration date of the commission, and when applicable, a photocopy of any police
report that specifies the theft; it should be sent immediately
Section 8206 (b) – Sequential journal; contents; thumbprint; loss of journal; copies of
pages; exclusive property of notary public; limitations on surrender .... Page 63

37. B. 20 days
Section 8204.1 – Cancellation of Commission; failure to pay; notice .... Page 60

38. D. A valid driver's license or identification card
Section 8230 (b) – Identification of affiant; verification.. Page 96

39. C. The type of document
Section 8206 (c) – Sequential journal; contents; thumbprint; loss of journal; copies of
pages; exclusive property of notary public; limitations on surrender .... Page 64

40. A. The signatures of the credible witnesses, type of identifying documents, identifying
numbers of the documents, and the dates of issuance or expiration of the documents
presented by the witnesses to establish their identities
Acknowledgment .... Page 18

PRACTICE TEST 5: ANSWER SHEET

1. Ⓐ Ⓑ Ⓒ Ⓓ   11. Ⓐ Ⓑ Ⓒ Ⓓ   21. Ⓐ Ⓑ Ⓒ Ⓓ   31. Ⓐ Ⓑ Ⓒ Ⓓ

2. Ⓐ Ⓑ Ⓒ Ⓓ   12. Ⓐ Ⓑ Ⓒ Ⓓ   22. Ⓐ Ⓑ Ⓒ Ⓓ   32. Ⓐ Ⓑ Ⓒ Ⓓ

3. Ⓐ Ⓑ Ⓒ Ⓓ   13. Ⓐ Ⓑ Ⓒ Ⓓ   23. Ⓐ Ⓑ Ⓒ Ⓓ   33. Ⓐ Ⓑ Ⓒ Ⓓ

4. Ⓐ Ⓑ Ⓒ Ⓓ   14. Ⓐ Ⓑ Ⓒ Ⓓ   24. Ⓐ Ⓑ Ⓒ Ⓓ   34. Ⓐ Ⓑ Ⓒ Ⓓ

5. Ⓐ Ⓑ Ⓒ Ⓓ   15. Ⓐ Ⓑ Ⓒ Ⓓ   25. Ⓐ Ⓑ Ⓒ Ⓓ   35. Ⓐ Ⓑ Ⓒ Ⓓ

6. Ⓐ Ⓑ Ⓒ Ⓓ   16. Ⓐ Ⓑ Ⓒ Ⓓ   26. Ⓐ Ⓑ Ⓒ Ⓓ   36. Ⓐ Ⓑ Ⓒ Ⓓ

7. Ⓐ Ⓑ Ⓒ Ⓓ   17. Ⓐ Ⓑ Ⓒ Ⓓ   27. Ⓐ Ⓑ Ⓒ Ⓓ   37. Ⓐ Ⓑ Ⓒ Ⓓ

8. Ⓐ Ⓑ Ⓒ Ⓓ   18. Ⓐ Ⓑ Ⓒ Ⓓ   28. Ⓐ Ⓑ Ⓒ Ⓓ   38. Ⓐ Ⓑ Ⓒ Ⓓ

9. Ⓐ Ⓑ Ⓒ Ⓓ   19. Ⓐ Ⓑ Ⓒ Ⓓ   29. Ⓐ Ⓑ Ⓒ Ⓓ   39. Ⓐ Ⓑ Ⓒ Ⓓ

10. Ⓐ Ⓑ Ⓒ Ⓓ   20. Ⓐ Ⓑ Ⓒ Ⓓ   30. Ⓐ Ⓑ Ⓒ Ⓓ   40. Ⓐ Ⓑ Ⓒ Ⓓ

PRACTICE TEST 5 QUESTIONS

1. Any officer appointed or elected in the state of California must take and subscribe an oath or affirmation which is found in:

    A. The local county clerk rules and procedures manual
    B. The United States Constitution
    C. The California Constitution
    D. The International Convention of Notaries Public

2. A person appearing on a principal's behalf to prove the principal signed the document is called:

    A. An attorney-in-fact
    B. A proxy
    C. A credible witness
    D. A subscribing witness

3. A fine of up to $750 may be issued to the notary for which of the following:

    A. Notarizing documents without being commissioned
    B. Acting as an attorney
    C. Failing to give the oath when required, failure to complete an acknowledgment at the time of notarization, charging more than the prescribed fees or negligent failure to perform duties required of a notary
    D. A and C

4. What is one reason the Secretary of State may refuse to appoint or revoke a notary public's commission?

    A. Failure to secure the official seal and sequential journal
    B. Charging less than the fee prescribed by law
    C. Reporting the loss of a sequential journal too late
    D. Not completing an acknowledgment at the time of seal and signature

5. What must notary public applicants submit to the Department of Justice?

    A. A list of state and federal convictions and arrests
    B. Fingerprint images and related information
    C. A record of state and federal arrests only
    D. A written request for a federal summary of criminal information

6. Which of the following situations does a notary public have a direct financial or beneficial interest in a transaction?

    A. When the notary public is acting as an agent for a person having a direct financial interest in the transaction
    B. When the notary public is named as a principal to a financial transaction
    C. When the notary public is named as a lender to a real property transaction

D. When the notary public is acting as an attorney for a person having a direct beneficial interest in the transaction

7. How long does a notary public have to respond to a written request sent by certified mail from any member of the public asking for information on official acts performed by the notary public?

   A. 15 business days
   B. 30 days
   C. Certified mail is not an authorized means of delivery
   D. 24 hours

8. The mandatory language in an enclosed box on a certificate of acknowledgment must legibly state:

   A. "A notary public or other officer completing this certificate verifies only the identity of the individual who signed the document to which this certificate is attached, and not the truthfulness, accuracy, or validity of that document."
   B. "A notary public or other officer completing this certificate verifies only the identity, age, and location of the individual who signed the document to which this certificate is attached, and not the truthfulness, accuracy, or validity of that document."
   C. "A notary public or other officer completing this certificate verifies only the identity of the individual by satisfactory evidence and the

apparent completeness of the document."
   D. "A notary public or other officer completing this certificate verifies the identity, address, age, and county of signature by the individual who signed the document to which this certificate is attached, and not the truthfulness, accuracy, or validity of that document."

9. For what purpose does the Secretary of State require notary public applicants to be fingerprinted?

   A. To confirm the applicant's identity
   B. To determine whether or not the applicant has been convicted of disqualifying crime
   C. Both of the above
   D. None of the above

10. What is prima facie evidence when a notary public, acting in the course of employment by a financial institution, protests a bill of exchange or promissory note for nonacceptance or nonpayment?

   A. The fact of presentment and its manner
   B. The time and place of protest
   C. The drawee or acceptor's address
   D. The notary's personal opinion

11. What is the required surety bond amount for a notary public?

   A. $15,000
   B. $15,000/$30,000/$5,000
   C. $25,000

D. None of the above

12. Thomas asks his friend Mark, who is a notary, to perform an illegal notary act and offers him money as a bribe. What is Mark guilty of?

A. Perjury
B. First-degree felony
C. Second-degree felony
D. Misdemeanor

13. What must a notary public immediately do if their official seal is lost, misplaced, destroyed, broken, damaged, or is rendered otherwise unworkable?

A. File a police report
B. Give the manufacturer/vendor of the original seal the broken or damaged seal and ask them to create another one
C. Mail or deliver written notice of the situation to the Secretary of State
D. Mail or deliver written notice of the situation to the county clerk where the notary public's oath and bond are filed

14. A subscribing witness must prove that the person who first signed the instrument is the person described in the instrument and:

A. The person who first signed the instrument is the same person described in the instrument
B. That the person who first signed the instrument signed it in the presence of the subscribing witness or stated

to the subscribing witness that he/she signed it
C. All of the above
D. None of the above

15. A certificate of authorization may be requested from:

A. The governor's office
B. The Department of Real Estate
C. The Secretary of State
D. None of the above

16. What is the term of office for a notary public?

A. Two years
B. Three years
C. Four years
D. Five years

17. What may the Secretary of State do to ensure consistency and compliance with the laws governing applicants and notaries public?

A. Adopt any additional rules or regulations necessary to effectively carry out the laws governing applicants and notaries public
B. Form and deploy a special task force to enforce all notary public laws
C. Both of the above
D. None of the above

18. The requirements for the oaths of two credible witnesses are:

A. Not allowed
B. Must be over 18 years old
C. Must be fingerprinted

D. None of the above

19. What is the definition of "price gouging"?

 A. Any practice that has the effect of pressuring a customer to pay for something he or she does not need
 B. Any practice that offers a certain product or service described in one way yet delivers a substandard, lesser quality product or service
 C. Any practice that has the effect of pressuring a client or prospective client to purchase services immediately for fear of having to pay more for the same services if they wait until later
 D. Any practice which charges a higher amount for discriminatory reasons against protected persons

20. Any person who knowingly files a forged deed of trust with a county recorder on real property consisting of a single-family residence containing no more than four dwelling units is punishable by, among other things, a fine not to exceed:

 A. $75,000
 B. $5,000
 C. $15,000
 D. $50,000

21. When you resign a commission, you deliver all your papers to:

 A. Secretary of State
 B. County Clerk where your current oath was filed

C. Your employer
D. None of the above

22. Can a private employer limit a notary public's services if they have an agreement with the employee?

 A. No, a notary public must provide notarial services for any transaction
 B. Yes, but only if the employer is a government agency
 C. Yes, but only if the employee is compensated for the notarial services they provide
 D. Yes, only if the employee agrees and the services are directly related to the employer's business

23. When is a notary public required to provide a receipt for fees collected on any notary act?

 A. Never
 B. Upon request of the customer for whom the notarial act was performed
 C. Always, no exceptions
 D. Only when the statutory fee amount exceeds the amount of $10

24. How long after the commencement of a notary public's commission does the notary public have to file an oath of office and official bond with the clerk of the county shown on the notary public's application?

 A. 30 days
 B. 15 business days
 C. 72 hours
 D. None of the above

25. A plea of nolo contendere ("no contest") is deemed by the Secretary of State to be:

A. An excusable act
B. A justifiable misdemeanor
C. A conviction
D. Neutral – neither "guilty" nor "not guilty"

26. Prior to the Secretary of State's suspension or revocation of a notary public's commission for violation of notary public laws, the applicant or notary public (choose one):

A. Has the right to a hearing
B. Has the right to a prorated refund of all fees paid by the notary public in obtaining their commission
C. May request a waiver from the state of California Attorney General
D. Shall avoid the imposition of monetary fines by voluntarily relinquishing their notary journal and official seal to the Secretary of State

27. A signature by mark is only valid if:

A. It is witnessed by at least one other person who also signs their own name
B. It is witnessed by at least two other people who also sign their names
C. It is witnessed by someone who must be personally known by both the notary public and by the person signing their name by mark
D. None of the above

28. Which of the following statements is/are true?

A. A notary public may notarize the affidavit of their own deposition as long as it only pertains to the notary public and no one else
B. A notary public is prohibited from taking proof of an instrument of writing executed by anyone to whom the notary public is related
C. Both of the above
D. None of the above

29. Maria is a notary public and is presented with a document to notarize. She realizes that the document is missing the signature of one of the parties involved. What should Maria do in this situation?

A. Refuse to notarize the document and explain why it is incomplete
B. Notarize the document anyway and sign the missing party's name herself
C. Ask the person presenting the document to sign the missing party's name and then notarize it
D. Notarize the document and ask the missing party to sign it at a later time

30. A certification from the Commission on Judicial Performance authorizing a retired judge or justice to administer oaths and affirmations is obtained by:

A. A finding by the Commission that the retired judge or justice was censured but not disbarred

B. A finding by the Commission through various methods that the retired judge or justice is mentally and physically fit to administer oaths or affirmations

C. A finding by the Commission that the retired judge or justice had at least 20 years of service on the bench

D. A finding by the Commission that the retired judge or justice is bilingual

31. A notary public completes a certificate of acknowledgment that contains statements they know to be false. What are the potential consequences?

    A. Civil penalties, administrative action, and criminal charges

    B. Civil penalties and administrative action only

    C. Criminal charges and administrative action only

    D. None of the above

32. A notary public charges a client $15 for notarizing a document, but tells the client that if they do not pay immediately, the price will be $30 tomorrow. What is the term for this practice?

    A. "Price hiking"

    B. "Price fluctuation"

    C. "Price inflation"

    D. "Price gouging"

33. Two credible witnesses can be used to establish the identity of a signer only if:

    A. The notary public knows at least one of the witnesses personally

    B. They both swear under oath that the signer cannot reasonably obtain another form of identification

    C. The witnesses have known each other personally for at least one year

    D. At least one of the witnesses is related to the signer

34. A private employer may only restrict a notary public from providing notarial services to any person(s) other than those directly associated with the business purposes of the employer if:

    A. The employer and notary public agree to the restriction for the duration of the notary public's employment

    B. The employer has no other notary public employees on staff

    C. The notary public is under the age of 21

    D. All of the above

35. It is a _____ when a Notary fails to properly maintain their journal. Fill in the blank.

    A. Misdemeanor

    B. Felony

    C. Imposed fine

    D. Violation

36. The statute of limitations for making a statement known to be false is:

A. One year
B. Two years
C. Three years
D. Four years

37. What is the Secretary of State's processing fee for an expedited address change?

    A. $15
    B. $50 plus return postage
    C. Free
    D. $10 if within the 30 day time limit, $25 if 31 days or more

38. What is the notary public required to do upon the request of their employer regarding their journal transactions?

    A. The notary public is required to allow their employer to inspect and copy all transactions in their journal, regardless of whether they are related to the employer's business
    B. The notary public is required to provide copies of all transactions in their journal, regardless of whether they are related to the employer's business
    C. The notary public is not required to allow their employer to inspect or copy any transactions in their journal
    D. The notary public is required to allow their employer to inspect and copy all transactions in their journal that are related to the employer's business

39. What happens to the commission when a notary public changes their name and completes a name change form?

    A. The commission term and commission number remains the same
    B. The commission term resets to the date the form was submitted and a new commission number is assigned
    C. The commission term remains the same but a new commission number is assigned
    D. The commission terminates

40. If a notary public is also an immigration specialist, the notary public may only advertise their notary services if:

    A. A prescribed notice, printed in English and the other language the notary public uses in advertising, is clearly posted
    B. The advertising does not contain the words "notario public" or "notario"
    C. A list of fees set by statute for notarial services is posted
    D. None of the above

PRACTICE TEST 5: ANSWER KEY

1. C. The California Constitution

Section 1360 – Necessity of taking constitutional oath .... Page 97

2. D. A subscribing witness

Proof of Execution by a Subscribing Witness .... Page 23

3. C. Failing to give the oath when required, failure to complete an acknowledgment at the time of notarization, charging more than the prescribed fees or negligent failure to perform duties required of a notary

Section 8214.15 (b) – Civil penalties .... Page 81

4. A. Failure to secure the official seal and sequential journal

Grounds for Denial Revocation of Appointment and Commission .... Page 37

5. B. Fingerprint images and related information

Section 8201.1 (b) – Additional qualifications; determination; identification .... Page 51

6. B. When the notary public is named as a principal to a financial transaction

Section 8224 (a) – Conflict of interest; financial or beneficial interest in transaction; exceptions .... Page 92

7. A. 15 business days

Section 8206.5 – Notaries; supplying photostatic copies on request; defending position in a disciplinary proceeding .... Page 66

8. A. "A notary public or other officer completing this certificate verifies only the identity of the individual who signed the document to which this certificate is attached, and not the truthfulness, accuracy, or validity of that document."

Section 1189 (a)(1) – Certificate of acknowledgment; form; sufficiency of out of state acknowledgment; force and effect of acknowledgment under prior laws .... Page 110

9. C. Both of the above

Section 8201.1 (a) – Additional qualifications; determination; identification .... Page 50

10. A The fact of presentment and its manner

Section 8208 – Protest of bill or note for nonacceptance or nonpayment .... Page 71

11. A. $15,000

Notary Public Bond .... Page 6

12. D. Misdemeanor

Section 8225 (a) – Improper notarial acts, solicitation, coercion or influence of performance; misdemeanor .... Page 93

13. C. Mail or deliver written notice of the situation to the Secretary of State

Section 8207.3 (e) – Certificates of authorization; authorization to provide seal; lost, misplaced, damaged or otherwise unworkable seal .... Page 69

14. C. All of the above

Section 1197 – Subscribing witness; items to be proved .... Page 116

15. C. The Secretary of State

Section 8207.3 (a) – Certificate of authorization; authorization to provide seal; lost, misplaced, damaged or otherwise unworkable seal .... Page 69

16. C. Four years

Section 8204 – Term of office .... Page 60

17. A. Adopt any additional rules or regulations necessary to effectively carry out the laws governing applicants and notaries public

Section 8220 – Rules and regulations .... Page 88

18. D. None of the above

Identification (C) .... Page 11

19. C. Any practice that has the effect of pressuring a client or prospective client to purchase services immediately for fear of having to pay more for the same services if they wait until later

Section 22449 (b)(2) – Deferred Action for Childhood Arrivals program; price gouging; penalties .... Page 133

20. A. $75,000

Section 115.5 – Filing false or forged documents relating to single-family residences; punishment; false statement to notary public .... Page 129

21. B. County Clerk where your current oath was filed

Section 8209 (a) – Resignation, disqualification or removal of notary; records delivered to clerk; misdemeanor; death; destruction of records .... Page 72

22. D. Yes, only if the employee agrees and the services are directly related to the employer's business

Section 8202.8 – Private employers; limitation on provision of notarial services .... Page 57

23. B. Upon request of the customer for whom the notarial act was performed

Section 6109 – Receipt of fees; written account; officer liability .... Page 100

24. A. 30 days

Section 8213 (a) – Bonds and oaths; filing; certificate; copy of oath as evidence; transfer to new county; name changes; fees .... Page 75

25. C. A conviction

Section 8214.1 (b) – Grounds for refusal, revocation of commission .... Page 79

26. A. Has the right to a hearing

Section 8214.3 – Hearing prior to denial or revocation of commission or imposition of civil penalties; law governing; exceptions .... Page 84

27. A. It is witnessed by at least one other person who also signs their own name

Section 14 – Words and phrases; construction; tense; gender; number .... Page 105

28. D. None of the above

Section 8224.1 – Writings, depositions, or affidavits of notary public; prohibitions against proof or taking by that notary public .... Page 92

29. A. Refuse to notarize the document and explain why it is incomplete

Notarization of Incomplete Documents .... Page 32

30. B. A finding by the Commission through various methods that the retired judge or justice is mentally and physically fit to administer oaths or affirmations

Section 2093 (c)(1-4) – Officers authorized to administer oaths or affirmations ... Page 121

31. A. Civil penalties, administrative action, and criminal charges

Acknowledgment .... Page 18

32. D. "Price gouging"

Section 22449 (c)(2) – Deferred Action for Childhood Arrivals program; price gouging; penalties .... Page 133

33. B. They both swear under oath that the signer cannot reasonably obtain another form of identification

Identification .... Page 10

34. A. The employer and notary public agree to the restriction for the duration of the notary public's employment

Section 8202.8 – Private employers; limitation on provision of notarial services .... Page 57

35. A. Misdemeanor

Notary Public Journal .... Page 15

36. D. Four years

Section 6203 – False certificate or writing by officer .... Page 101

37. C. Free

Change of Address .... Page 41

38. D. The notary public is required to allow their employer to inspect and copy all transactions in their journal that are related to the employer's business

Section 8206 (d) – Sequential journal; contents; thumbprint; loss of journal; copies of pages; exclusive property of notary public; limitations on surrender .... Page 64

39. A. The commission term and commission number remains the same

40. D. None of the above

PRACTICE TEST 6: ANSWER SHEET

1. Ⓐ Ⓑ Ⓒ Ⓓ　11. Ⓐ Ⓑ Ⓒ Ⓓ　21. Ⓐ Ⓑ Ⓒ Ⓓ　31. Ⓐ Ⓑ Ⓒ Ⓓ

2. Ⓐ Ⓑ Ⓒ Ⓓ　12. Ⓐ Ⓑ Ⓒ Ⓓ　22. Ⓐ Ⓑ Ⓒ Ⓓ　32. Ⓐ Ⓑ Ⓒ Ⓓ

3. Ⓐ Ⓑ Ⓒ Ⓓ　13. Ⓐ Ⓑ Ⓒ Ⓓ　23. Ⓐ Ⓑ Ⓒ Ⓓ　33. Ⓐ Ⓑ Ⓒ Ⓓ

4. Ⓐ Ⓑ Ⓒ Ⓓ　14. Ⓐ Ⓑ Ⓒ Ⓓ　24. Ⓐ Ⓑ Ⓒ Ⓓ　34. Ⓐ Ⓑ Ⓒ Ⓓ

5. Ⓐ Ⓑ Ⓒ Ⓓ　15. Ⓐ Ⓑ Ⓒ Ⓓ　25. Ⓐ Ⓑ Ⓒ Ⓓ　35. Ⓐ Ⓑ Ⓒ Ⓓ

6. Ⓐ Ⓑ Ⓒ Ⓓ　16. Ⓐ Ⓑ Ⓒ Ⓓ　26. Ⓐ Ⓑ Ⓒ Ⓓ　36. Ⓐ Ⓑ Ⓒ Ⓓ

7. Ⓐ Ⓑ Ⓒ Ⓓ　17. Ⓐ Ⓑ Ⓒ Ⓓ　27. Ⓐ Ⓑ Ⓒ Ⓓ　37. Ⓐ Ⓑ Ⓒ Ⓓ

8. Ⓐ Ⓑ Ⓒ Ⓓ　18. Ⓐ Ⓑ Ⓒ Ⓓ　28. Ⓐ Ⓑ Ⓒ Ⓓ　38. Ⓐ Ⓑ Ⓒ Ⓓ

9. Ⓐ Ⓑ Ⓒ Ⓓ　19. Ⓐ Ⓑ Ⓒ Ⓓ　29. Ⓐ Ⓑ Ⓒ Ⓓ　39. Ⓐ Ⓑ Ⓒ Ⓓ

10. Ⓐ Ⓑ Ⓒ Ⓓ　20. Ⓐ Ⓑ Ⓒ Ⓓ　30. Ⓐ Ⓑ Ⓒ Ⓓ　40. Ⓐ Ⓑ Ⓒ Ⓓ

PRACTICE TEST 6 QUESTIONS

1. A certificate of acknowledgment taken in any other state or jurisdiction besides California is:

   A. Insufficient in the state of California and must be notarized again by a notary public of competent jurisdiction and good standing in the state of California
   B. Sufficient as long as it's okay by the state or jurisdiction where it was taken
   C. Sufficient as long as the resident is presently a resident of the state of California
   D. Insufficient unless accompanied by a letter or statement by the original witness to the signed instrument including their telephone number and commission number/expiration

2. What should the personal representative of a deceased notary public do?

   A. Notify the Secretary of State and deliver records to county clerk
   B. Notify the county clerk and deliver records to the Secretary of State
   C. Notify the Secretary of State and deliver records to the deceased's family
   D. None of the above

3. If a notary public discovers an error in a completed notarial act, what should they do?

   A. Cross out the error and initial it, then have the signer initial it, and attach a new certificate containing the correct information
   B. Nothing can be done to correct a completed notarial act according to the law
   C. Notarize the signature on the document again, completing and attaching a new certificate containing the date of the new notarial act and completing a new journal entry
   D. Notify the signer of the error and have them correct it before a new notarial act can be performed

4. Which one of the following items is not required to be included on a notary public's official seal?

   A. The notary public's name
   B. The notary public's date of commission by the Secretary of State
   C. The State Seal
   D. The county where the notary public's oath and bond are filed

5. The Commission on Judicial Performance may charge a regulatory fee in the amount of $_____ for each certification application it receives. Fill in the blank.

   A. $15
   B. Not more than $25
   C. Not less than $25
   D. Not more than $2,500

6. If a notary public is found guilty of price

gouging when a client or prospective client requests services associated with filing an application for deferred action for childhood arrivals, he/she is subject to:

A. Suspension or revocation of their commission by the Secretary of State
B. Imprisonment in county jail for a period not to exceed 6 months
C. No penalty
D. None of the above

7. Which of the following is not a reason for the Secretary of State to refuse appointing an applicant or notary public or terminating/revoking/suspending the commission of a notary public?

A. Omitting information about a prior conviction on the application for appointment as a notary public
B. Notarizing any instrument containing a statement(s) the notary public knows to be false
C. Failure to obtain a signer's thumbprint in the notary journal after he/she executes an employment contract
D. Failure to keep the notary journal and official seal locked and accessible to only the notary public

8. What can a notary public in California do for documents filed in another state or jurisdiction?

A. Complete a certificate of acknowledgment required in another state
B. Make determinations and certificates

allowed by California law
C. Certify that the signer holds a particular capacity
D. Refuse to acknowledge a document from another state

9. When a check has not been honored for payment, the Secretary of State shall give a written notice. How many days after the first notice will a second notice be given if no payment was made?

A. 10 days
B. 20 days
C. 40 days
D. 90 days

10. Mark is a notary public, an officer of the Navy, a United States citizen, and over 17 years old. How can Mark be appointed as a notary public for the Navy?

A. Be recommended by the commanding officer of the Navy
B. Be recommended by the commanding officer of any branch within the Armed Forces of the United States
C. Submit a formal request to the Secretary of State
D. Mark can already provide notarial services within the boundaries of the Navy

11. The county named in the heading of a notarial certificate is:

A. The county where the notary public's oath and bond are filed
B. The county where the person is

signing the document

C. The county where the notary public's principal place of business is located

D. The county shown on the notary public's official seal

12. The maximum fee for notarizing a circulator's affidavit is:

A. No Fee
B. $7.00
C. $10.00
D. $15.00

13. The Secretary of State must approve any course of study proposed by a vendor to ensure the course of study includes which of the following?

A. The date and time of the next written examination
B. The Secretary of State's contact information
C. All material a person is expected to know to adequately complete the written examination
D. All locations where the course of study may be attended

14. What is the fine for failing to notify the Secretary of State of a lost, broken or damaged seal?

A. $750
B. $1,500
C. $2,000
D. $2,500

15. What is the punishment for knowingly failing to notify the Secretary of State of a name change?

A. First-degree felony
B. Second-degree felony
C. Infraction
D. Infraction and a possible fine of up to $500

16. When presented with a document written in a foreign language the notary public does not understand, the notary public:

A. Must reject the document and refuse to notarize anything he/she cannot read and understand
B. Must contact a translator who can read the document to the notary public
C. Does not have to understand what the document says as long as it is looks complete
D. Is required to refer the signer to an attorney

17. Which of the following items is not required to be recorded in a notary journal?

A. The time of day the notarial act happened
B. The amount of any fee charged by the notary public
C. How the fee was paid (cash, check, or credit/debit card)
D. The signer's thumbprint under special circumstances

18. When do you officially become a notary?

A. When you do your first certificate

B. When the Secretary of State sends your commission

C. When you pass the exam

D. When your oath and bond are filed

19. Which of the following statements is true?

   A. If a notary public's principal place of business changes counties, he/she must file a new oath and bond in the new county

   B. If a notary public's principal place of business changes counties he/she must immediately obtain an updated official seal reflecting the name of the new county

   C. If a notary public's principal place of business changes counties, he/she is not required to file a new oath and bond in the new county

   D. If a notary public's principal place of business changes counties, the notary public must submit an application to the Secretary of State for a new commission

20. Which one of the following items is required for the Secretary of State to appoint and commission a notary public for a military reservation?

   A. Provide the Secretary of State with a DD-214 if the appointee is a veteran

   B. Be at least 21 years of age

   C. Obtain a certificate of approval from the U.S. Department of Defense

   D. Be a citizen of the United States

21. Which action(s) constitute forgery?

   A. Making, altering, or counterfeiting a document with the intent to defraud

   B. Passing a document knowing it to be false

   C. Falsifying the acknowledgment of any notary public

   D. All of the above

22. In a disciplinary proceeding for noncompliance, what defense may a notary use for delayed action in response to a request for a copy of a transaction?

   A. The notary may not defend their delayed action under any circumstances

   B. The notary may only defend their delayed action on the basis of unavoidable business circumstances

   C. The notary may only defend their delayed action on the basis of personal circumstances

   D. The notary may defend their delayed action on the basis of unavoidable, exigent business or personal circumstances

23. If a notary public is found to have committed official misconduct or neglect, who is liable?

   A. The notary public

   B. The sureties on the notary public's official bond

   C. No party can be held liable

   D. A and B

24. A California notary can always:

   A. Advertise they are immigration consultants

B. Take depositions and affidavits

C. Certify a copy of a foreign birth certificate

D. Issue confidential marriage licenses

25. Which of the following is NOT a reason for revoking a notary public's commission?

    A. Properly completing the acknowledgment at the time the notary public's seal and signature are attached to the document

    B. Charging more than the fee prescribed by law

    C. Failure to submit to the Secretary of State any court ordered money judgment

    D. Making a false certificate or writing containing statements known to be false

26. If a notary public shreds their notary journal when it is full instead of filing it with the county clerk, the notary public is:

    A. Guilty of a felony subject to a fine of no more than $2,500

    B. Guilty of a misdemeanor and liable for payment of damages to anyone injured by the notary public's actions

    C. Subject to official administrative reprimand and suspension of their commission for no more than 90 days

    D. Not subject to any disciplinary action

27. Who may assist a person with immigration forms?

A. A representative accredited by the U.S. Department of State

B. A person registered with the California Department of Justice and bonded as an immigration consultant under the Business and Consultants Code

C. Both of the above

D. None of the above

28. If any payment made to the Secretary of State by a notary public or applicant is returned unpaid, how should the applicant or notary public remit the replacement payment?

    A. Credit or debit card

    B. Cashier's check or money order

    C. Personal check

    D. Cash only

29. A proof or acknowledgement of an instrument may be made before:

    A. A notary public but only within the county where their principle place of business is located

    B. A sitting judge located anywhere in the state of California

    C. A notary public anywhere in California

    D. All of the above

30. Unless it is otherwise allowed, an oath may be taken in front of:

    A. Any officer authorized to administer oaths

    B. Any officer authorized to administer oaths in a local court of competent jurisdiction

C. Any officer authorized to administer oaths in a state, county, or municipal law enforcement department

D. Any person of suitable age and competency

31. An electronic signature is satisfactory for any instrument requiring a notarized signature as long as:

A. The electronic signature is accompanied by the electronic signature of the notary public

B. All parties to the instrument agree to the electronic signature

C. Written approval is obtained by the Secretary of State

D. The instrument is filed with the local county clerk after execution

32. Anyone who bullies a notary public to notarize something that the notary public shouldn't be notarizing is guilty of:

A. A class felony

B. A misdemeanor

C. An administrative reprimand

D. Assault

33. A notary public will avoid investigation and disciplinary proceedings by the Secretary of State if the notary public:

A. Obtains a waiver from the state of California Attorney General

B. Has a valid sales tax license

C. Voluntarily resigns their commission before the Secretary of State begins the investigation

D. None of the above

34. After a notary public has received a fee for performing a notarial act, the notary public must:

A. Determine whether or not the instrument is complete

B. Determine whether or not the signer's identity is true and accurate

C. Determine whether or not the signer's identification is valid

D. Perform the notarial act or risk being liable upon their bond

35. What will the Secretary of State do with the list of approved course providers?

A. Distribute it with the laws of California relating to notaries public

B. Keep the list confidential

C. Only provide it upon request

D. Notify the notary public commission of all approved providers

36. What is the maximum civil penalty for tampering with the identification number on the notarial seal?

A. $1500

B. $2500

C. $1000

D. $5000

37. The identity of a subscribing witness must be established through the oath of a credible witness who:

A. Personally knows both the principal and the notary public

B. Personally knows both the subscribing witness and the notary public

C. Personally knows the principal and the subscribing witness

D. All of the above

38. Acceptable ID's must be current or issued within:

A. 1 year

B. 2 years

C. 5 years

D. 10 years

39. A person who, sworn under oath to tell the truth, deliberately states something he/she knows to be false is guilty of what crime?

A. Forgery

B. Felony fraud

C. Perjury

D. All of the above

40. What is a possible penalty for a notary public who fails to perform their duties willfully?

A. A warning letter

B. Suspension of license

C. A misdemeanor charge

D. A monetary fine

PRACTICE TEST 6: ANSWER KEY

1. B. Sufficient as long as it's okay by the state or jurisdiction where it was originally taken
   Section 1189 (b) – Certificate of acknowledgment; form; sufficiency of out of state acknowledgment; force and effect of acknowledgment under prior laws .... Page 111

2. A Notify the Secretary of State and deliver records to county clerk
   Section 8209 (b) – Resignation, disqualification or removal of notary; records delivered to clerk; misdemeanor; death; destruction of records .... Page 72

3. C. Notarize the signature on the document again, completing and attaching a new certificate containing the date of the new notarial act and completing a new journal entry
   Correcting a Notarial Act .... Page 33

4. B. The notary public's date of commission by the Secretary of State
   Section 8207 – Seal .... Page 66

5. A. $15
   Section 2093 (c)(6) – Officers authorized to administer oaths or affirmations ...... Page 121

6. A. Suspension or revocation of their commission by the Secretary of State
   Section 22449 (c)(2) – Deferred Action for Childhood Arrivals program; price gouging; penalties .... Page 133

7. C. Failure to obtain a signer's thumbprint in the notary journal after he/she executes an employment contract
   Section 8214.1 (a)(l)(o) – Grounds for refusal, revocation of commission .... Page 79

8. A. Complete a certificate of acknowledgment required in another state
   Acknowledgment .... Page 18

9. B. 20 days
   Section 8204.1 – Cancellation of Commission; failure to pay; notice .... Page 60

10. A. Be recommended by the commanding officer of the Navy
    Section 8203.2 – Military and naval reservations, recommendation of commanding officer; jurisdiction of notary .... Page 58

11. B. The county where the person is signing the document
    Geographic Jurisdiction .... Page 6

12. A. No Fee
    Section 8080 – Fees for verification .... Page 125

13. C. All material a person is expected to know to adequately complete the written examination
    Section 8201.2 – Review of course of study for notary public; approval of education

PRACTICE TEST 7: ANSWER SHEET

1. Ⓐ Ⓑ Ⓒ Ⓓ   11. Ⓐ Ⓑ Ⓒ Ⓓ   21. Ⓐ Ⓑ Ⓒ Ⓓ   31. Ⓐ Ⓑ Ⓒ Ⓓ

2. Ⓐ Ⓑ Ⓒ Ⓓ   12. Ⓐ Ⓑ Ⓒ Ⓓ   22. Ⓐ Ⓑ Ⓒ Ⓓ   32. Ⓐ Ⓑ Ⓒ Ⓓ

3. Ⓐ Ⓑ Ⓒ Ⓓ   13. Ⓐ Ⓑ Ⓒ Ⓓ   23. Ⓐ Ⓑ Ⓒ Ⓓ   33. Ⓐ Ⓑ Ⓒ Ⓓ

4. Ⓐ Ⓑ Ⓒ Ⓓ   14. Ⓐ Ⓑ Ⓒ Ⓓ   24. Ⓐ Ⓑ Ⓒ Ⓓ   34. Ⓐ Ⓑ Ⓒ Ⓓ

5. Ⓐ Ⓑ Ⓒ Ⓓ   15. Ⓐ Ⓑ Ⓒ Ⓓ   25. Ⓐ Ⓑ Ⓒ Ⓓ   35. Ⓐ Ⓑ Ⓒ Ⓓ

6. Ⓐ Ⓑ Ⓒ Ⓓ   16. Ⓐ Ⓑ Ⓒ Ⓓ   26. Ⓐ Ⓑ Ⓒ Ⓓ   36. Ⓐ Ⓑ Ⓒ Ⓓ

7. Ⓐ Ⓑ Ⓒ Ⓓ   17. Ⓐ Ⓑ Ⓒ Ⓓ   27. Ⓐ Ⓑ Ⓒ Ⓓ   37. Ⓐ Ⓑ Ⓒ Ⓓ

8. Ⓐ Ⓑ Ⓒ Ⓓ   18. Ⓐ Ⓑ Ⓒ Ⓓ   28. Ⓐ Ⓑ Ⓒ Ⓓ   38. Ⓐ Ⓑ Ⓒ Ⓓ

9. Ⓐ Ⓑ Ⓒ Ⓓ   19. Ⓐ Ⓑ Ⓒ Ⓓ   29. Ⓐ Ⓑ Ⓒ Ⓓ   39. Ⓐ Ⓑ Ⓒ Ⓓ

10. Ⓐ Ⓑ Ⓒ Ⓓ   20. Ⓐ Ⓑ Ⓒ Ⓓ   30. Ⓐ Ⓑ Ⓒ Ⓓ   40. Ⓐ Ⓑ Ⓒ Ⓓ

PRACTICE TEST 7 QUESTIONS

1. What is the purpose of transferring civil penalties collected to the General Fund?

    A. To be used for notary public training programs
    B. To be distributed to the county where the violation occurred
    C. To defray Secretary of State's office costs in investigating notary public law violations
    D. To fund the state's public defender system

2. The notary stamp may be:

    A. Rectangular
    B. Triangle
    C. Circular
    D. A & C

3. A notary public has an obligation to perform which of the following duties?

    A. To take the acknowledgment or proof of power of attorney and provide a certificate of that proof or acknowledgment either on the power of attorney itself or attached to it
    B. Sign any deposition, affidavit, oath, or affirmation in their own handwriting
    C. Both of the above
    D. None of the above

4. When establishing the identity of a signer, what is not needed on the identification document?

    A. Picture of the signer

B. Signature of the signer
C. Notary's signature
D. Identifying number

5. If the law requires a record to be retained in its original form, it is:

    A. Mandatory to keep the original physical copy of the record on file
    B. Okay to keep an electronic version of the record and shred the original physical copy
    C. A good idea to provide the original physical copy of the record to an attorney or safe deposit box for safekeeping
    D. None of the above

6. Which of the following is a requirement for a protest made by a notary public?

    A. It can be made upon unsatisfactory information
    B. It must be made outside the course and scope of employment
    C. It must identify the instrument and certify presentment or reasons why it was not made
    D. It cannot certify that notice of dishonor has been given to any party

7. What is the responsibility of a notary public when executing a jurat?

    A. Determine satisfactory evidence and administer an oath or affirmation
    B. Witness the signing of the document only

C. Determine the legal validity of the document
D. Provide legal advice to the affiant

8. A notary public who wishes to obtain authorization to issue confidential marriage licenses must:

A. Consult the Secretary of State
B. Apply to the Secretary of State
C. Complete a course of instruction on issuing confidential marriage licenses
D. Be approved by the Secretary of State

9. What services are exempted from notary fees for U.S. military veterans?

A. Any legal documents
B. Only documents affecting real property
C. All notarial services
D. Only pension, compensation, and other veterans benefits applications

10. Which of the following may be administered by obtaining an affirmative response to the following question: "Do you solemnly state that the evidence you shall give in this issue (or matter) shall be the truth, the whole truth, and nothing but the truth, so help you God?"

A. An oath
B. An affirmation
C. A declaration
D. All of the above

11. The fine for willful failure to notify the Secretary of State of an address or name change is:

A. $500
B. $750
C. $1,500
D. $15,000

12. When completing a signature by mark, under what circumstances must the notary verify the identity of the document principal?

A. Only when the two witnesses also are used as credible witnesses
B. If one witness is used as a credible witness and is personally known to the notary
C. Never
D. Always

13. What is required of non-attorney notary publics who advertise notarial services in a language other than English in California?

A. They must post a notice in English and the other language stating they are not an attorney and cannot give legal advice about immigration or any other legal matters
B. They must list the fees set by statute that a notary public may charge for notarial services
C. They cannot translate the term "Notary Public" into Spanish, even if they have posted the required notice
D. All of the above

14. What is the maximum diameter of an embosser-type seal?

A. 2.5 inches
B. 1.75 inches

C. 2 inches

D. 3 inches by 3 inches with a milled border

15. Which of the following actions can the Secretary of State take when reviewing a notary public application or a notary public commission?

   A. Deny a notary public application for unpaid child support

   B. Suspend a notary public commission for traffic violations

   C. Approve a notary public application without background check

   D. Allow a notary public commission even with outstanding family support obligations

16. Officers of the state, county, or any judicial district shall not perform a notarial act unless:

   A. The officer receives the payment of the fee prescribed by law

   B. The officer waives the statutory fee that could otherwise be collected

   C. The officer obtains written permission from the Secretary of State to waive a fee that should otherwise be collected

   D. The officer receives any fee amount he/she wishes to charge

17. What are the requirements for proof of execution by a subscribing witness?

   A. The subscribing witness must identify the principal, witness their signature, and sign the notary public's journal

   B. The notary public must personally

know the credible witness

   C. The subscribing witness must identify the principal and personally know them

   D. The subscribing witness must identify the notary public

18. When the Secretary of State revokes a notary public's commission, what must be done with the notice of revocation?

   A. It is posted for three consecutive weeks in any periodical that is published or circulated in the county where the notary public's oath and bond are on file

   B. It is filed with the county clerk where the notary public's oath and bond are on file

   C. It is mailed to the notary public's employer via first class certified mail, return receipt requested

   D. All of the above

19. Which of the following acts by a notary public may be considered the practice of law?

   A. Determining, based upon their experience, whether a document is complete or incomplete before being signed

   B. Requiring an affiant to raise their right hand and take an oath promising the truth, whole truth, and nothing but the truth for a deposition

   C. Warning a signer that her divorce paperwork package is incomplete before she signs the documents

   D. Certifying the photocopy of a Power of Attorney as accurate with their signature and official seal

20. Any civil penalties collected pursuant to Section 8214.15. of the Government Code shall be transferred to:

A. The State of California Department of Justice
B. The General Fund
C. The Notary Public Licensing Bureau
D. The California Department of Tax and Fee Administration

21. The protest of a bill or note for nonacceptance or nonpayment by a notary public acting within the scope of their employment with a financial institution is prima facie evidence of the facts recited therein if which one of the following is specified by the notary public on said protest:

A. The length of time the notary public has been employed with the financial institution;
B. The cause or reason for protesting the bill
C. The name and address of the chief financial officer for the financial institution where the notary public is employed
D. The county in which the financial institution is located

22. If a notary public cannot determine the type or title of a document in a foreign language, he/she may:

A. Do nothing and just write "a document written in a language I don't understand" in their notary journal
B. Require the signer to bring a translator who will read and explain the document to the notary public
C. Allow the signer to complete the acknowledgment or jurat form and show the notary public where to sign and affix their seal
D. None of the above

23. If an instrument is signed by Elise, a Delaware corporation's assistant secretary, Elise's signature means:

A. It may be considered an authorized act of the Delaware corporation
B. It may not be considered an authorized act of the Delaware corporation
C. It may be considered an authorized act of the Delaware corporation's secretarial division
D. It may be considered personally binding upon the assistant secretary, but not the corporation

24. A notary public may not be appointed to a military reserve if:

A. The appointee lives in a different county than the military reserve
B. The commanding officer of the reserve has not made a recommendation for the appointment
C. The appointee is less than 21 years of age
D. None of the above

25. What is the consequence of failing to pay for the examination, application,

commission, and fingerprint fee for a notary public?

A. The notary public will be fined $500 for each violation
B. The notary public will be given a warning
C. The notary public will be required to retake the examination
D. The Secretary of State may cancel the commission of the notary public

26. What must a notary public's official seal contain?

A. The name of the notary and the date the notary public's commission expires
B. The name of the notary, the State Seal, and the words "Notary Public"
C. The name of the notary, the State Seal, the words "Notary Public", and the name of the county wherein the bond and oath of office are filed
D. The name of the notary, the State Seal, the words "Notary Public", and the sequential identification number assigned to the notary

27. If a notary public applies to the Secretary of State for a name change, he/she has 30 days after the amended commission is issued to do which of the following?

A. Update their business cards
B. Update their official seal
C. File their notary public journal with the county clerk where the notary public's principal place of business is located and start a new notary journal

D. File a new oath and amended bond with the county clerk where the notary public's principal place of business is located

28. A person who falsely claims to be a notary public may be:

A. Guilty of a felony
B. Reprimanded but not charged
C. Guilty of an aggravated felony if he/she actually signs something
D. Guilty of a misdemeanor

29. A person may not be found guilty of perjury if proof of the person's false statement(s) under oath is:

A. Discovered more than four years after the false statements were made
B. Discovered more than two years after the false statements were made
C. Based solely upon the contradicting testimony of a person other than the defendant
D. Not witnessed by at least two other persons

30. If the Secretary of State has reason to believe a person is violating or intends to violate the rules, regulations, and laws governing notaries public and notary public applicants, the Secretary of State has the authority to:

A. Conduct surveillance on the person(s) to catch them in the act
B. Suspend the suspect's driver's license until the investigation is complete
C. Apply for an injunction
D. Both A and C

31. If you lost your certificate of authorization and have provided the Secretary of State written notice, when will the Secretary of State issue you a new certificate of authorization?

A. One month
B. 5 working days
C. One year
D. 30 working days

32. A notary can certify a copy of a power of attorney according to the:

A. Civil Code
B. Probate Code
C. Bus. & Prof. Code
D. Notary Public Code

33. Which one of the following is not an officer who may take a proof or acknowledgment of an instrument?

A. A city clerk
B. A police officer within their municipal jurisdiction only
C. A district attorney
D. A retired judge of a municipal or justice court

34. What information on the Secretary of State's application for appointment and commission as a notary public is not confidential?

A. The applicant's gender
B. The applicant's full name and address
C. The applicant's age
D. The applicant's level of education

35. For a person's mark in a notary public journal to qualify as a signature, it must:

A. Be witnessed by a person who then writes the signer's name next to the mark
B. Be accompanied by the thumbprint of the person making their mark
C. Be witnessed by the notary public and include the notary public's signature
D. Be witnessed by no less than two witnesses who must also sign the notary public journal

36. A notary changing their name (due to a marriage, for example) must:

A. Submit an application with the Secretary of State for a name change
B. File a new oath of office and an amendment to the bond within 30 days
C. Obtain a Certificate of Authorization to manufacture a new seal with the new name
D. All of the above

37. How many days does a notary public have to respond to a letter from any member of the public requesting a copy of a transaction which may be in the notary public's journal?

A. 15
B. 30
C. 10 business days (not including holidays or weekends)
D. There is no prescribed time period, just within a reasonable turnaround time

38. A notary who executes a jurat on an instrument he/she knows to contain false statements or information is guilty of:

D. None of the above

A. A felony
B. Conspiracy
C. A misdemeanor
D. Forgery

39. Which of the following is true regarding the performance of official services by state officers or county officers?

A. They are prohibited from performing any official services
B. They may perform official services without charging any fees
C. They may only perform official services if the fees are remitted to the state or public agency
D. They may perform official services only upon the payment of the fees prescribed by law

40. An oath or affirmation is administered by obtaining an affirmative answer to the following question:

A. "Do you swear to tell the truth, the whole truth, and nothing but the truth so help you God?"
B. "Do you solemnly state under penalty of perjury that you are telling the truth?"
C. "Do you solemnly state under penalty of perjury that the evidence you shall give in this issue shall be the truth, the whole truth, and nothing but the truth?"

PRACTICE TEST 7: ANSWER KEY

1. C. To defray Secretary of State's office costs in investigating notary public law violations
Section 8214.15 (d) – Civil penalties .... Page 81

2. D. A & C
Section 8207 – Seal .... Page 66

3. C. Both of the above
Section 8205 (a) – Duties .... Page 61

4. C. Notary's signature
Section 1185 (1)(A) – Acknowledgments; requisites .... Page 106

5. B. Okay to keep an electronic version of the record and shred the original physical copy
Section 1633.12 (d) – Retaining records; electronic satisfaction .... Page 118

6. C. It must identify the instrument and certify presentment or reasons why it was not made
Section 3505 (b) – Protest; Noting for Protest .... Page 126

7. A. Determine satisfactory evidence and administer an oath or affirmation
Section 8202 – Execution of jurat; administration of oath or affirmation to affiant;
attachment to affidavit .... Page 53

8. C. Complete a course of instruction on issuing confidential marriage licenses
Confidential Marriage Licenses .... Page 36

9. D. Only pension, compensation, and other veterans benefits applications
Section 8211 – Fees .... Page 73

10. D. All of the above
Section 2094 – Oath to witness; form .... Page 123

11. A. $500
Section 8213.6 – Name changes; application; filing .... Page 77

12. D. Always
Signature by Mark .... Page 28

13. D. All of the above
Illegal Advertising .... Page 34

14. C. 2 inches
Section 8207 – Seal .... Page 66

15. A. Deny a notary public application for unpaid child support
Grounds for Denial Revocation of Appointment and Commission .... Page 37

16. A. The officer receives the payment of the fee prescribed by law
Section 6100 – Performance of services; officers; notaries public .... Page 97

17. A. The subscribing witness must identify the principal, witness their signature, and sign the notary public's journal

18. B. It is filed with the county clerk where the notary public's oath and bond are on file

19. C. Warning a signer that her divorce paperwork package is incomplete before she signs the documents

20. B. The General Fund

21. B. The cause or reason for protesting the bill

22. A. Do nothing and just write "a document written in a language I don't understand" in their notary journal

23. A. It may be considered an authorized act of the Delaware corporation

24. B. The commanding officer of the reserve has not made a recommendation for the appointment

25. D. The Secretary of State may cancel the commission of the notary public

26. C. The name of the notary, the State Seal, the words "Notary Public", and the name of the county wherein the bond and oath of office are filed

27. D. File a new oath and amended bond with the county clerk where the notary public's principal place of business is located

28. D. Guilty of a misdemeanor

29. C. Based solely upon the contradicting testimony of a person other than the defendant

30. C. Apply for an injunction

Section 8222 – Injunction; reimbursement for expenses

31. B. 5 working days

Section 8207.3 (e) – Certificates of authorization; authorization to provide seal; lost, misplaced, damaged or otherwise unworkable seal

32. B. Probate Code

Powers of Attorney – Certifying

33. B. A police officer within their municipal jurisdiction only

Section 1181 – Notaries public; officers before whom proof or acknowledgment may be made

34. B. The applicant's full legal name and address

Section 8201.5 – Application form; confidential nature; use of information

35. A. Be witnessed by a person who then writes the signer's name next to the mark

Signature by Mark

36. D. All of the above

Section 8213 (c) – Bonds and oaths; fling; certificate; copy of oath as evidence; transfer to new county; name changes; fees

37. A. 15

Notary Public Journal

38. C. A misdemeanor

Section 6203 (a) – False certificate or writing by officer

39. D. They may perform official services only upon the payment of the fees prescribed by law

Section 6100 – Performance of services; officers; notaries public

40. C. "Do you solemnly state under penalty of perjury that the evidence you shall give in this issue shall be the truth, the whole truth, and nothing but the truth?"

Section 2094 – Oath to witness; form

TRUE OR FALSE: ANSWER KEY

1. **FALSE**

   Multiple requirements must be satisfied before an applicant can become a notary public, including fingerprinting and a background check.

2. **FALSE**

   Any convictions, which includes misdemeanors, must be reported on the Applicant's application for the Secretary of State's review and consideration.

3. **TRUE**

   Every Applicant wishing to be appointed as a notary public must attend and complete an approved six-hour course of study at least once.

4. **TRUE**

   A notary public's commission becomes invalid if the required oath and bond have not been properly filed by the notary within 30 calendar days.

5. **TRUE**

   The bond is not an insurance company to protect the notary public from financial loss. The bond is held to financially compensate the public from any wrongful acts of the notary public and the notary public is personally responsible for reimbursing the bonding company.

6. **FALSE**

   A notary public commissioned in the state of California may perform notarial acts anywhere within the state of California.

7. **FALSE**

   A notary public cannot draft, select, or advise any person on legal documents and processes.

8. **TRUE**

   A notary public must ensure the information on the seal is accurate, that it imprints clearly when used, and it is securely locked away when not being used.

9. **FALSE**

   A single credible witness swearing to another person's identity must personally know the notary public AND present at least one satisfactory identification document.

10. **FALSE**

    A notary public may maintain only one sequentially-numbered journal at any time.

11. **TRUE**

    If the notary public does not stand to gain from a document being signed by a relative or personal acquaintance, the notary public may notarize their signature.

12. FALSE

In a certificate of acknowledgment, the notary public is certifying that the signer personally appeared before the notary public on that date, in that county, proved their identity, and acknowledged their signature of the document.

13. TRUE

A jurat is completed by the notary public only after the signer has verbally sworn or affirmed to the notary public that the contents of the document are true and accurate.

14. FALSE

A subscribing witness must only provide the document needing notarization and a credible witness who knows both the subscribing witness and the notary public.

15. TRUE

Two witnesses must subscribe a person's mark on a document, but they are only confirming they witnessed that person make their mark. The witnesses are not confirming the person's identity.

16. FALSE

The notary public must have the original power of attorney to examine before he/she may certify the copy as true and accurate.

17. FALSE

Under no circumstances may a notary public notarize any document that is incomplete or missing data.

18. FALSE

Any correction of a notarial act requires the notary to do correct the mistake and perform a new notarization on the document as if it were the first time.

19. FALSE

A notary may only certify the truth and accuracy of a copy of power of attorney.

20. TRUE

A notary public may notarize immigration paperwork for a signer but any questions the signer may have about the documents must be referred to an immigration specialist or an attorney.

21. FALSE

A notary public may offer and advertise their services as an immigration specialist or consultant, but he/she may not disclose their status as a notary public.

22. FALSE

Approval to issue confidential marriage licenses is made at the discretion of the county clerk and the notary public may or may not be approved.

23. FALSE

The Secretary of State may refuse to appoint a person or suspend/revoke a notary public's active commission at its discretion for infractions which may not be listed above.

24. TRUE

The Secretary of State's disciplinary guidelines protect a notary applicant or notary public from inconsistent, biased, or unfair treatment in notary disciplinary matters.

25. FALSE

A notary public may never charge a fee for notarial acts if he/she is appointed to a military or naval reservation.

26. FALSE

The notary public is permitted to provide notarial services anywhere in the state, regardless of where their oath of office and bond are on file.

27. TRUE

The notary public is only required to validate a signer's identity and willful intent to sign, not the content of the document.

28. FALSE

The notary public is permitted to provide notarial services anywhere in the state, regardless of where their oath of office and bond are on file.

29. TRUE

The Secretary of State commissions notaries public as it sees fit to maintain convenience for the public to access notarial services.

30. FALSE

A renewal applicant may only take the three-hour refresher course if he/she has previously completed a six-hour study course and their commission is current.

31. TRUE

The Department of Justice and the FBI require an applicant's fingerprints and personal information to execute a statewide and nationwide search for any criminal records.

32. FALSE

A notary public study course MUST be approved by the Secretary of State with a certificate of approval before being offered to the public.

33. TRUE

The Department of Justice and the FBI require an applicant's fingerprints and personal information to execute a statewide and nationwide search for any criminal records.

34. FALSE

The language in the notice box of a jurat must be exactly as quoted above and the language must also be enclosed in a box located at the top of the jurat.

35. FALSE

A notary public must maintain exclusive, secure possession of their seal and all notary journal(s) at all times and must not relinquish possession of either to an employer or former employer regardless of the government agency.

36. FALSE

The private employer and notary public employee must enter into a mutual agreement regarding the employer's payment of said expenses and the notary public's remittance of fees to the employer.

37. FALSE

The private employer and notary public employee must enter into a mutual agreement regarding the employer's payment of said expenses and the notary public's remittance of fees to the employer. Said agreement is only valid and enforceable for the duration of the notary public's employment with that employer

38. FALSE

A person can only be appointed as a notary public on military and naval reservations within the state of California.

39. FALSE

No applicant is automatically approved by the Secretary of State under any circumstances. All applicants must be able to comply with the prescribed rules and regulations for appointment as a notary public.

40. TRUE

In addition to mandatory compliance with all other criteria for appointment and commission as a notary public, the applicant must also be a federal civil service employee working at that military/naval reservation.

41. TRUE

As long as the notary public remains employed at the military/naval reservation where he/she is appointed, the notary may renew their commission multiple times in four-year increments as long as the notary remains qualified and in good standing with the Secretary of State and obtain the commanding officer's recommendation for each term.

42. FALSE

Once a notary public's payment has been rejected by the financial institution, the notary public must replace it with a cashier's check or a similar guaranteed payment method.

43. FALSE

The notary public must have the original power of attorney to examine before he/she may certify the copy as true and accurate.

44. FALSE

A notary public must always be present when their notary journal is being examined and copied.

45. TRUE

A notary public has a duty to provide a copy of a transaction in their notary journal, or written confirmation that the requested information does not exist, or the notary may face disciplinary action.

46. FALSE

A notary public must destroy their seal upon expiration or termination of their commission and ensure the seal is completely unusable and illegible.

47. FALSE

The Secretary of State assigns each notary public an identification number which is issued in consecutive numeric order, not by name.

48. TRUE

Once a vendor has complied with the rules and guidelines prescribed by the Secretary of State, the vendor shall receive a permit authorizing that vendor to manufacture and sell notary public seals to anyone with a valid certificate of authorization.

49. TRUE

Every authorized vendor is required to maintain a photocopy record of each certificate of authorization and its identification number received by the vendor for the manufacture of an official notary seal.

50. TRUE

Anyone who purposely violates these Sections can be punished with more than monetary penalties.

51. TRUE

A notary public's statement of the reason for protesting the instrument is accepted as obvious truth of the facts stated in the protest.

52. FALSE

Upon a notary public's death, the executor or personal representative of the notary's estate must contact the Secretary of State and deliver all notarial records and documents to the county clerk where the notary's oath and bond were filed.

53. TRUE

A notary public may charge what he/she wishes for notarial fees, or charge nothing at all, but may never exceed the maximum fee amounts prescribed by Section 8211.

54. TRUE

A notary public's commission becomes invalid if the required oath and bond have not been properly filed by the notary within 30 calendar days.

55. FALSE

A notary public may only use the address of a commercial mail receiving agency as their place of business only if the notary has provided the Secretary of State with a valid physical address for their residence.

56. FALSE

The term of the commission will remain the same when a notary public who gets their name change form approved by the Secretary of State.

57. FALSE

The notary public can be sued personally for compensation as well as the surety bond.

58. TRUE

Any offense by a notary public which results in the revocation of a notary's professional licensing is grounds to have their commission revoked by the Secretary of State.

59. TRUE

If no hearing has been requested in a disciplinary action no hearing officer is necessary, therefore, the Secretary of State may impose any penalty(ies) prescribed by law.

60. TRUE

If the notary public knows the deed of trust for real property with a single family home built on it is improper in any way and he/she proceeds to notarize it for gain of any kind, he/she is guilty of a felony.

61. FALSE

If a peace officer asks to review a notary public's journal, the notary must provide it to the peace officer or be subject to a fine of no more than $2,500.00.

62. FALSE

A notary public is required to obtain a signer's thumbprint on any power of attorney and failure to do so is punishable under this section.

63. FALSE

The notary public is not entitled to a hearing less than one year after their application was denied or commission revoked; or if the Secretary of State has entered an order finding the notary public or applicant has committed or omitted certain disqualifying violations.

64. TRUE

The Secretary of State may investigate a notary public's actions, make findings, and enter orders imposing penalties as appropriate regardless of the notary's commission status.

65. TRUE

The Secretary of State must provide notice and documentation of a notary public's commission revocation to the county clerk.

66. TRUE

The court shall require the notary public to surrender their official seal if the court has revoked their commission.

67. FALSE

A surety must first apply to the superior court in the county where the notary public's main place of business is located and then serve the application and notice of hearing upon the Secretary of State.

68. TRUE

A notary public may notarize immigration paperwork for a signer but any questions the signer may have about the documents must be referred to an immigration specialist or an attorney.

69. TRUE

The Secretary of State may adopt rules and regulations at its own discretion to carry out the duties of its office.

70. FALSE

While the person who shredded the notary journal may avoid prosecution and penalty by this Section, he/she may still be prosecuted under different laws with different (or no) time limits for prosecution.

71. TRUE

The Secretary of State may petition a court to impose an injunction or restraining order upon a person, but the person has the right to appeal the injunction or order to have it dissolved.

72. FALSE

A notary public may offer and advertise their services as an immigration specialist or consultant, but he/she may not disclose their status as a notary public.

73. TRUE

If the notary public does not stand to gain from a document being signed by a relative or personal acquaintance, the notary public may notarize their signature.

74. TRUE

The provisions of this code do not prevent the prosecution of the person under different laws with different (or no) time limits for prosecution and with different charges and penalties.

75. FALSE

Anyone besides an appointed, commissioned notary public who identifies as a notary public is guilty of a misdemeanor.

76. TRUE

It is a misdemeanor crime to misrepresent oneself as a notary public if the person is not a notary public, but it is a felony offense for a person to act as a notary public in any transaction that creates a debt on a single-family home.

77. TRUE

Upon reasonable suspicion, any peace officer or agent of the Secretary of State are authorized to examine a notary public's journal, papers, or other evidence of official acts.

78. TRUE

If a notary keeps their seal in an unsecured place where it can be accessed by others besides the notary public, that person is guilty of a misdemeanor.

79. FALSE

Any document other than immigration-related documents which states the age and birthdate of the signer must be verified by the notary public with a certified copy of the signer's birth certificate or an ID/driver's license issued by the Department of Motor Vehicles.

80. FALSE

A notary public may be required to charge a fee for their notarial services and remit the collected funds to their employer.

81. FALSE

A notary public may never charge a fee for notarial services rendered to someone securing a pension, regardless of the notary's employer or obligation to collect fees for that employer.

82. FALSE

A notary public may not charge or collect a fee for notarizing or certifying any document for a US Armed Forces veteran which may be related to a veteran's application for, eligibility determination, or any other purpose relating to veteran's benefits for the veteran. The notary may charge a fee to the veteran for notarizing any other instruments unrelated to securing military benefits or pensions.

83. TRUE

A notary public may not charge or collect any fee(s) for administering or certifying the oath of a public official.

84. TRUE

A receipt detailing the services rendered by a notary public and the fee for providing those services may be necessary for the notary public to provide.

85. FALSE

A notary is never required to notarize an incomplete or otherwise insufficient instrument. The notary must refund the fee that was paid and reject the incomplete document.

86. TRUE

A notary public must be confident that the instrument is true and accurate to the best of the notary's knowledge or the notary public must refuse to notarize and issue it.

87. FALSE

The signer on a deed of trust must prove their identity to the notary public with satisfactory evidence.

88. TRUE

A notary public does not need to affix their seal to a finalized map as long as the notary's name, county of business, and commission expiration date are written next to the notary's signature.

89. TRUE

Two witnesses must subscribe a person's mark on a document, but they are only confirming they witnessed that person make their mark. The witnesses are not confirming the person's identity.

90. TRUE

A document signer may verify their identity and signature on the document to a notary public anywhere in the state. There are other officers who may do it instead of a notary public, but only in the county or city/county where the officer was elected or appointed.

91. FALSE

A single credible witness swearing to another person's identity must personally know the notary public AND present at least one satisfactory identification document.

92. TRUE

When a certificate of acknowledgment is endorsed by a notary public, it must either be printed on the instrument itself or attached to the instrument if it is on a separate piece of paper.

93. FALSE

In a certificate of acknowledgment, the notary public is certifying that the signer personally appeared before the notary public on that date, in that county, proved their identity, and acknowledged their signature of the document.

94. FALSE

In a certificate of acknowledgment for an entity, the notary public is simply vouching for the confirmed identity of the person signing the document. The notary may rely on the signer's claim to be the duly authorized person for the entity, in the absence of any evidence that would suggest otherwise.

95. FALSE

A certificate of acknowledgment that is signed by a notary public must affix their official seal to the instrument as well.

96. TRUE

A power of attorney must be signed before the notary public and may not be acknowledged to the notary after the fact for a certificate of proof.

97. FALSE

The identity of a witness who subscribes a document may only be verified by the oath of another person ("a credible witness") who is able to provide the notary public with appropriate identification.

98. TRUE

The subscribing witness isn't swearing to the content of the instrument, only the fact that he/she knows the signer, knows the document pertains to the signer, that he/she watched the signer sign the document, and that he/she also signed the document as a witness.

99. FALSE

The digital data attached to the party's electronic signature must include the notary public's electronic signature, just as if it was a physical signature on a document.

100. FALSE

The requirement to retain the electronic copy of the contract does not include the addresses, names, or other information that was used solely to send and receive the document.

101. TRUE

A subscribing witness is anyone, including friends or family members, who sees a written execution or hears an acknowledgment.

102. TRUE

The Commission on Judicial Performance is the body responsible for investigating and determining a former judge's or justice's qualifications and suitability for administering oaths and affirmations.

103. FALSE

It is not necessary for a person being placed under oath to raise their right hand.

104. FALSE

Under no circumstances may a notary public charge for verifying a nomination document or circulator's affidavit, regardless of the notary's employer.

105. FALSE

A notary public employed by a financial institution needs to check if the evidence provided is reasonable and satisfactory. If the notary executes a false protest because he was not satisfied as to the evidence presented, the notary may be held liable.

106. TRUE

The authorized person certifying a copy of a power of attorney must be able to compare it to the original.

107. TRUE

While a felony is punishable by incarceration in a state prison (or county jail for certain specific reasons), a misdemeanor may also be punishable by incarceration in a city jail for a year or less.

108. TRUE

True, and in addition to criminal charges arising from the felony charges, the person is also subject to a fine of no more than $75,000.00.

109. TRUE

If the only evidence of a person lying under oath is testimony by another person who says they lied, the evidence is insufficient and the accused shall not be convicted.

110. FALSE

For the act of copying someone else's signature, mark, or seal to be defined as forgery, the person who copied the signature, mark, or seal must do so with the specific intent to commit fraud.

111. FALSE

A notary public is one of only four agents or class of agents as named in Section 22449 who are actually permitted to charge a fee for notarial services.

Made in the USA
Las Vegas, NV
24 November 2023